# Squirrel
# WARS

# Squirrel
# WARS

## Backyard Wildlife Battles
## & How to Win Them

by George H. Harrison

Edited by Kit Harrison

Willow Creek Press

P R E S S

MINOCQUA, WISCONSIN

Photography Credits / Copyrights:
All photographs by George H. Harrison except as follows:
John J. Lainson, page 12; Joyce Lund, p. 18, 46; Jay Joyner, p. 26; Droll
Yankees Inc., pgs. 29, 136; Duncraft, pgs. 30, 31, 137;
Dean & Sherry Johnson, p. 32; Paul Benzer, p. 34; Beth Funston, p. 40;
Hal H. Harrison, pgs. 47, 138, 142; Harold P. Bone, p. 48;
Woody Hagge, pgs. 84, 86; Garrett Long, p. 87; Ted Levin/Animals
Animals, p. 106; Marilyn Burkhart, p. 120; TC Nature/Animals
Animals, p. 124; Parks, P. OSF/Animals Animals, p. 126;
C.C. Lockwood/Animals Animals, p. 169.

Published by Willow Creek Press
P.O. Box 147, Minocqua, Wisconsin 54548
For information on other Willow Creek Press titles,
call 1-800-850-9453


Library of Congress Cataloging-in-Publication Data
Harrison, George H.
    Squirrel wars : backyard wildlife battles and how to win them / by
George H. Harrison ; edited by Kit Harrison.
        p. cm.
    ISBN 1-57223-298-6
    1. Mammal pests--Control. 2. Bird pests--Control. 3. Garden
pests--Control. I. Harrison, Kit. II. Title.

SB993.5 .H37 2000
635.9'29--dc21                                           00-022002


Printed in the United States

# Table of Contents

## ACKNOWLEDGMENTS

A special thanks to the editors and readers of *Birds & Blooms*, *Birder's World*, *Wild Bird* and *Bird Watcher's Digest*, who live with the problems of backyard wildlife pests, as exemplified by the many anecdotes that were theirs.

Thanks, too, to various friends who related their "War Stories"—Jack and Mary Ann Brendel, Olive Hazlett, Lloyd LaRoque, Ed and Jean LeRoy, Tom Schwartz, Jim and Jane Surpless, John Forester, Frank and Pat Dentice, Bob and Nancy Barton, Michael Furtman, Jay and Lorraine Cassell, and many more.

In some cases, names have been changed at the request of the individuals to protect their privacy. Many thanks to them, too, for sharing their dilemmas and remedies.

And, finally, thanks to the gray squirrels, whose backyard antics made this book possible. Surely, life in the backyard without those damnable squirrels would be oh so dull.

# The Battlefield

Deep in a suburb in the middle of America lives a typical American family. Let's call them the Jones family. They always enjoyed the birds and other wildlife they spotted on seasonal outings to the local nature center, occasional visits to the zoo and on vacation trips to national parks and refuges. If fact, they got so much pleasure from observing nature, particularly the birds, that they decided to create a wildlife habitat in their own backyard.

The whole family participated in the planning and planting of the prescribed trees, shrubs, flowers and ground cover that was recommended for attracting a variety of wildlife. They installed a recirculating pool in which the birds could drink and bathe, and worked together to mount bird feeders on posts, hang them from tree limbs, and secure them to the trunks of big trees.

In a short time they had created a model wildlife habitat that rewarded them with almost instant results. For example, no sooner had they put up the hopper feeder than a band of chickadees arrived to check it out. The newly installed tray feeder had just been filled with sunflower seeds when the first cardinal flew in for a snack, followed by a nuthatch and a goldfinch. The pond, with its adjacent shelter of freshly planted greenery, was suddenly a busy place—with robins, blue jays, and rose-breasted grosbeaks waiting in line for a dip and a sip.

With a little hard work, along with a nominal invest-
ment, the Jones family had created a wildlife paradise right
outside their windows. It would get better and better as
time went on and the new plantings matured.

The euphoria of watching the beautiful birds fluttering
from feeder to feeder began to fade, though, as soon as the
first gray squirrel shinnied up the pole and into the hopper
feeder. The Joneses had nothing against squirrels at this
point and were actually amused as they watched the greedy
squirrel crack and eat dozens of sunflower seeds in short
order. However, they realized almost immediately that the
squirrel aggressively prevented the cardinal and the chickadee from getting the food. The bushytail became increas-
ingly comfortable in its new home, gobbling up large
quantities of cracked corn and sunflower seed meant for
the birds.

A chubby little chipmunk found the tray feeder around
the same time and spent its days filling its pudgy cheek

pouches with seed, repeatedly disappearing down a hole in the ground and returning in a flash to refill its cheeks.

For a while, the Joneses endured the daily visits from squirrels and chipmunks, although as the number of raiding animals continued to grow, the Joneses' tolerance declined.

Late one afternoon a few months later, as dusk settled on the Joneses' backyard habitat, a small herd of deer wandered in and began munching on the tender young shrubbery, eating many of the fresh sprouts down to the roots. After trimming the shrubbery, the deer moved on to the impatiens, then the begonias.

Shortly after dark the following week, a commotion at the feeders was illuminated when the motion-sensing outdoor patio light came on. A family of raccoons was working its way through the offerings. Having knocked down the hopper feeder and the tray feeder, two of the raccoons were now suspended from a limb and eating from the hanging feeder.

One night, a skunk joined the fray, followed by an opossum, both vacuuming up the birdseed that had fallen to the ground. Then a rat arrived.

Paradise was lost. Many mornings, the bird feeders were on the ground, empty, and damaged or destroyed by four-footed backyard visitors. The lovingly planted shrubs and flowers were nearly gone, having been eaten back to their stubs by deer and rabbits.

The Jones family was devastated. The nature center hadn't mentioned that their backyard wildlife might possibly include not only the lovely birds that pleased them so greatly, but also an army of pest animals that would leave their garden and feeding station looking like a battlefield at the end of a war.

The reality of any successful backyard wildlife habitat is that the word "wildlife" means all wildlife, not just lovely birds and butterflies. It is just as likely to appeal to a

platoon of pest animals, because the same high-quality food, water and natural cover that attracts cardinals, chickadees, goldfinches and downy woodpeckers also attracts gray squirrels, chipmunks, white-tailed deer, bears, raccoons, skunks, and bully birds like starlings, grackles and pigeons.

Of course, some people genuinely enjoy all of these creatures and are just as content to see a squirrel or two as they are to glimpse a tanager or hummingbird.

The Joneses' reaction is more typical, however. They now spend a great deal of time and energy attempting to keep the squirrels, rabbits, and other unwanted animals off the feeders and out of the bird baths. In fact, their efforts to foil the pests sometimes verge on being ridiculous and outrageous.

In the end, like everyone else, the Joneses have three options. The first is to give up the whole idea of a backyard wildlife habitat and stop feeding the birds altogether. Yet this is not a sensible option, because the joy and fulfillment of a successful backyard habitat far outweigh the aggravation of a few pests.

The second option is to live with the pests, and enjoy all the wildlife, both desirable and undesirable, offering the nuisance species their food and cover in areas that are separate from the celebrities' domain. It may be argued that the environs belonged to all these creatures long before the Jones family built a house there.

The third option is to control the pests by excluding, repelling, or removing them, or by manipulating food, cover and water to discourage them.

In my own backyard wildlife habitat, I have problems with the same pests that invaded the Joneses' habitat. Gray squirrels, chipmunks and raccoons have been particularly troublesome. To counterattack them and others, I have used a combination of options, deciding to live with some species—hawks, rabbits, skunks, deer, opossums, woodpeckers and bully birds—and taking aggressive action against others. In battles against squirrels, chipmunks and raccoons, I have trapped-and-transferred as well as installed effective baffles. In combat with rats, which we had during two of the last 30 years, I was particularly firm, removing as many as I could. We have not been visited by bears yet, but they are getting closer.

That's what this book is all about: the pests that backyard wildlife habitats attract, the strange things people have done to control them, and how to bring some peace to the battlefield.

*George H. Harrison*
*Hubertus, Wisconsin*

# SQUIRRELS

# The Problem with Squirrels

PUBLIC ENEMY NUMBER ONE in America's backyards is a one-pound busybody with industrial-strength teeth and a luxuriously bushy tail: the gray squirrel.

While killer bees and marauding bears occasionally capture headlines, the gray squirrel has been quietly destroying the infrastructure of the nation's backyards, vandalizing homes, sabotaging American business and assaulting innocent bystanders. It is the number one suspect in half of all unsolved fires, the acknowledged perpetrator in most nonweather-related power failures and the wire chomper responsible for twice bringing stock trades on the NASDAQ to a halt.

Weber, the grill manufacturer, estimates that 20 percent of all gas grill owners have had to replace a squirrel-chewed hose.

In Waterville, Ohio, a squirrel looking for a handout went on a rampage and bit a dozen people, including a UPS man.

Transgressions like these, along with innumerable variations of the gray squirrel's errant ways, make this rascal the prime generator of revenue in the pest-control industry. It is also responsible for the $4-million-a-year business in squirrel-proof bird feeders.

Author's Note: Though this chapter pertains specifically to gray squirrels, the information and advice can be applied to other tree squirrels in North America, which includes red squirrels and fox squirrels.

The gray squirrel is the prime generator of revenue in the pest-control industry.

The consequence of the widespread exasperation over squirrels sometimes manifests itself in all-out war in many American backyards and gardens, as gray squirrels test the mettle of human intelligence and endurance. Challenged by a gray, four-footed, furry beast, people have nearly gone berserk in their attempts to outwit, outmaneuver, out-think, and outperform gray squirrels. Some people have dedicated all of their free time to the task of "keeping those blasted squirrels off the feeders." Yet, gray squirrels continue to wreak havoc in backyards from coast to coast while the search for the perfect squirrel-proof bird feeder forges on. There seems a better chance that a cure for AIDS or cancer will be achieved first.

Why are there so many gray squirrels in the backyards of America? "We humans are providing better living conditions with bird food and bigger trees in our yards than squirrels can find in the wild," said Vagn Flyger, professor emeritus, University of Maryland, who has studied gray squirrels for 50 years.

Why are gray squirrels winning the war of wits, despite the best efforts of mankind? Because it is a biological fact that squirrels have more time and a greater motivation (their own survival) to devote to the fight, regardless of how long it takes.

Gray squirrels are the greatest paradox of all backyard wildlife. On the one hand, they are aggressive, destructive, persistent, annoying pests. On the other hand, they are intelligent, inquisitive, skillful, handsome and among the most interesting creatures to observe in the backyard. That explains why there are two camps of squirrel people: Those who genuinely hate gray squirrels and will do almost anything to rid their backyards of the nuisance, and those who genuinely enjoy watching them and are willing to spend a great deal of time and money keeping them well fed.

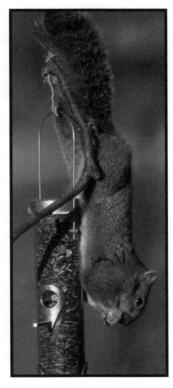

Squirrels frustrate many bird lovers by their uncanny ability to plunder even the most unreachable bird feeders.

Whether you are among those who love them or those who hate them, gray squirrels are here to stay. For those who can't accept that, the burning question, the ultimate challenge, the gold medal of backyard Olympics remains: perfecting a truly squirrel-proof bird feeder.

# War Stories

✳ Encouraged by bird-watcher friends, Ed and Jean LeRoy set up their first bird feeder in their New Berlin,

Squirrels in bird feeders not only chase all of the pretty songbirds away, but they also gobble up the seed in a fraction of the time.

Wisconsin, backyard. It was a hopper-type feeder mounted on a metal post. Their excitement over the prospects of attracting beautiful songbirds to their backyard was short-lived when a "cute" gray squirrel emptied the feeder even before the first bird arrived. After refilling it, the LeRoys watched a female cardinal try to land on the feeder, but she was forced to veer off when the gluttonous squirrel threatened her.

By the second day, the LeRoys were hosting a squirrel convention—seven bushytails, and counting. Having heard about squirrel baffles, Ed quickly purchased one from the same lawn-and-garden center that sold him the feeder. It kept the squirrels at bay for only five minutes after Ed attached it. The crafty animals found that they could jump onto the feeder from a nearby tree limb.

Ed moved the feeder. But no matter where he put it in his yard, the squirrels could jump onto it from a tree limb. So Ed started cutting tree limbs. The squirrels then jumped from the tree trunk. Ed cut down the tree. The squirrels jumped to the feeder from another tree farther away. Ed cut down that tree, too. Then the squirrels learned how to pull down the side of the baffle and climb over it. Ed built a better baffle that would not bend, but the squirrels learned how to jump to the top of the feeder from the ground. An exten-sion was added to the post, though it didn't elevate the feeder enough. At last report, the LeRoys were still feeding squirrels and not many birds. They were giving serious con-sideration to building a moat around the feeders and stock-ing it with piranhas.

A squirrel baffle won't work if the feeder is too close to a tree from which a squirrel can jump.

✳ A gray squirrel in a back-yard in Blacksburg, Virginia, jumped from a tree toward a bird feeder 47 times without success. On the 48th attempt, the squirrel landed squarely on the feeder. The squirrel never missed again.

✳ At the Schlitz Audubon Center in Milwaukee, a bird-seed study was to be conducted to determine the food preferences of the different species of birds in the area. A dozen bird feeders were strung on a wire, each filled with a different kind of seed. The study was immediately jeopard-ized by a horde of local gray squirrels that gobbled up the experimental seed before the birds could get to it. The gray squirrels preferred sunflower seeds 2:1 over all others until it was gone, then they ate all the other seeds.

The Audubon researchers tried to foil the squirrels by stringing beads, coffee cans and plastic milk bottles at both ends of the wire to keep the squirrels off the feeders. That failing, they set up large plastic walls at both ends of the wire, but the squirrels soon learned to leap over the plastic walls, land on the rolling coffee cans and do their balancing act all the way to the feeders. The birdseed experiment was abandoned.

※ Not far away from the Audubon Center, another backyard birder was initially successful in outwitting the squirrels by threading pie pans at each end of the horizontal wire on which his feeders hung. The frustrated squirrels finally learned to shake the wire, rocking the feeders until seed was knocked to the ground, where they had easy access to it.

※ One squirrel admirer learned a dear lesson from feeding his wild pets in the kitchen of his summer and weekend retreat. He allowed the gray squirrels to follow him inside, where they were invited to eat peanuts and birdseed from the kitchen storage bin. This was a great thrill to the

Squirrels may come to expect a handout once they've been fed.

The wooden end of this feeder was no match for the industrial-strength teeth of a gray squirrel.

weekender until he arrived at his cottage one Friday night to find that the squirrels had not waited for his return. They had chewed their way into the cottage and helped themselves to the bin of food.

✳ Even the president of the United States has squirrel problems. One spring, the gray squirrels in Lafayette Square, the little park across the street from the White House, ate 2,000 of the President's geraniums, girdled and killed over a half dozen newly planted trees and seriously injured some 100-year-old oaks.

✳ A Pennsylvania newspaper reported the adventure of a local woman who went outside to put her suitcase in the trunk of her car as she was leaving for her vacation. Since she needed both hands to manipulate the heavy suitcase, she didn't close the kitchen door on her way to the car, although she went back to shut it before going. When she returned from her trip, she phoned the police to report damage to the inside of her house, including ruined cabinets and other woodwork. After an investigation, the local police concluded that a squirrel had entered the open kitchen door and chewed the cabinets. The motive—food. Damage to the woodwork inside her house was more than $1,000. At last report, no suspects had been apprehended.

Although plenty cute, the gray squirrel will monopolize bird feeders unless strategic action is taken.

✳ Lloyd had endured about all he could take from the squirrels that had been plaguing his feeding station. He had tried a few tactics to keep the squirrels off, but one particularly fat one was back again with what Lloyd interpreted as a smirk on its whiskers, filling its chops with birdseed.

Now at the end of his rope, Lloyd got out his 12-gauge shotgun, slid open the patio door and took a shot. Amazingly, Lloyd missed the squirrel completely. The startled animal leaped off the feeder and disappeared up a tree.

Ten minutes later, the squirrel was back, greedily stuffing himself with birdseed. Lloyd slid the door open again, aimed and pulled the trigger. This time, the gun jammed and there was no shot.

Frustrated, Lloyd pointed the barrel downward and jerked the bolt action several times, when all of a sudden the gun fired, blowing a substantial hole in the living room carpet—which had been installed the previous day—and on through the flooring. A visiting kid, playing in the back of the house, shouted out in jest, "I'm hit, I'm hit," causing even more alarm for poor Lloyd, who by this time was frantic.

Meanwhile, the squirrel had returned after scurrying away from the noise of the floor shot and was again sitting on the feeder, contentedly enjoying a meal of Lloyd's finest birdseed.

Hopeless? Not at all. The trick is merely to find the appropriate solution for the circumstances.

# Solutions

## SHOCK THEM

Among the most consistently successful squirrel-proof bird feeders are those with built-in electrical shocking devices to keep away squirrels and raccoons. The most popular model is the WildBills® bird feeder. Its battery-operated charger lightly zaps squirrels when they make contact with plates and perches at the top and bottom of the feeder. Birds do not get a shock because, with only two legs, they cannot make a contact. The charge is strong enough to startle squirrels but not strong enough to hurt them. Yet it appears that it takes only one shock for a squirrel to get the message and give up trying to get the seed in a WildBills. My test feeder remains squirrel-free after several years.

The downside of the feeder is that it is expensive to purchase and requires high maintenance. Some talented people, therefore, build their own squirrel zappers.

### Squirrel Zapper Trains Man

❀ "My father hated the squirrels for eating the sunflower seeds he placed on the deck ledge for his feathered friends," said Jill Kusba of Oconomowoc, Wisconsin. "All his attempts to keep the squirrels away failed.

"Being a good daughter, I took it upon myself to find a solution. A shopping trip to the local hardware store did the trick," she said. "Copper wire, copper strips, plus an electric fence zapper were the essentials needed to construct a system that would deliver a negative reinforcement for the squirrels each time they approached the sunflower seeds. Eventually, they would learn to stay clear of the birds' food," Jill surmised.

"I rigged the copper strips along the deck railing far enough apart so that birds could not make contact and get a mild electric shock, but close enough together so that the four-legged squirrels would," she explained. "The wiring from the electric fence unit was brought inside the door and connected to a convenient wall switch.

"When my dad saw the first unsuspecting squirrel approach his bird food, he walked over to the switch and waited," she said. "The squirrel ran along the deck railing, as usual, toward the bird food. With conquest in his blood, my dad turned on the switch. Zap! The squirrel jumped straight up and then off the deck," Jill related.

"The squirrel was visibly upset with this new revelation. Tail up, twitching and chattering loudly, the furry bandit took a few moments to reassess the situation," she said.

"Confused but unharmed, the squirrel returned repeatedly to the railing, each time walking slower and slower, looking about for the culprit causing this nasty change in the feeding route. Eventually, the squirrel made the association of the man next to the window and the electric shock," Jill explained.

"After that, the race was on between man and squirrel. When the squirrel spotted my dad nearing the window, it would run the railing to beat him to the switch," she related. "Determined not to lose this battle to a squirrel, my dad would sprint for the window switch whenever he saw the squirrel approaching. The competition was fierce, but the squirrel was winning the race most often. This forced my dad to revert to crawling across the floor under the window each time the squirrel approached, surprising the squirrel all over again," Jill said.

"In only a few days, the squirrel had my dad trained to this new behavior of crawling on his hands and knees below the window. I guess, in his way, my dad had passed the squirrel's own intelligence test," she laughed.

❀ A couple in Chevy Chase, Maryland, were nearly at their wit's end with the squirrels in their backyard, according to an article in the *New York Times*, until they, too, concocted a way to utilize electricity. They attached copper tubing to the roof of their bird feeder and wired it into the house current. Birds continued to freely sit on the perches of the feeder, but any squirrel that jumped onto the feeder visited only once. The jolt they got didn't do them any harm but it was strong enough to send them into the air. Obviously, the experience was unpleasant enough that they didn't want to repeat it.

## BAFFLE THEM

The method used most often to keep squirrels off bird feeders is to baffle them with devices above and/or below the feeders. Baffles are usually metal or plastic tubes, disks or cans that are mounted on the post under the feeder, which stops squirrels from climbing up the post and onto the feeder. Likewise, a

Squirrels will simply slip off a plastic baffle like this one, with a steep slope and deep arch. Bird-watching is also unobstructed by the clear plastic.

These feeders are protected by baffles from above and below. If a baffle is not deep enough or wide enough, a squirrel will simply crawl over it and eat to its delight.

dome-shaped baffle above the feeder keeps squirrels from climbing down onto the feeder from above. Though baffles are readily available at bird stores, hardware and lawn-and-garden centers, they can also be fashioned at home. None of them, however, will keep squirrels off feeders unless the feeders are located at least six feet off the ground and at least ten feet away from trees, to keep squirrels from jumping over the baffles and directly onto the feeders.

### Garbage Can

❀ "We tried many feeders and many different ways to outsmart the squirrels, but just got frustrated," said Sally

Schofield of Port Richey, Florida, in *Birds & Blooms* magazine. "Finally, my husband, Don, said, 'Enough is enough!' He came up with the idea of taking a galvanized garbage can, painting it and mounting it upside-down well above the ground on the feeder pole. It was pretty funny to watch," Sally recalls. "The four-legged critters could climb up the pole and into the garbage can, but when they hit the roof, they couldn't get at the food in the feeder," she said.

## Sheet Metal

❀ Paul York was fed up with squirrels raiding the bird feeder in his rural New Hampshire backyard. At the local newspaper office, he purchased a sheet of the aluminum the paper uses for printing plates. From this, he fashioned a squirrel baffle by bending the plate into the appropriate shape and nailing it under his post-mounted bird feeder. It stopped not only squirrels, but raccoons as well and the materials cost less than a dollar.

❀ Many people have found that a length of aluminum duct keeps feeders squirrel-free. Larry Jenkins, of St. Louis, is one of them. He gets the aluminum duct at a hardware store for just a few dollars per section, fabricates it into a round sleeve simply by snapping it together and then installs it under the feeder. "The squirrels go up the post and into the duct, but no farther," he said.

## Slinky

❀ "I declared victory in the 'squirrel war' years ago," Ken Vail of Quincy, Illinois, told *Birder's World* magazine. "For about four dollars, I have enjoyed 99 percent squirrel-proof feeders. To do so, I attached one end of a Slinky® to the top of the pole and allowed the rest to hang so that the pole runs up through the center of the Slinky. Squirrels are stymied as they try to climb the pole. Typically, they will try to jump onto the pole, grab the Slinky and be promptly dumped to the ground. The one percent failure is represented by one squirrel, a fat buck fox squirrel who had obviously dined at bird feeders before. His first attempts to climb the pole failed. Then, to my astonishment, I watched as he put his nose under the Slinky and pushed it ahead of him as he climbed the pole. When he was up high enough, he jumped over to one of the suspended feeders." Ken said. He found that tying a string from the bottom of the Slinky to a brick on the ground solved that problem.

### Inverted Pot

❀ "My mobile bird feeder is protected from squirrels by a plastic flowerpot, which is placed upside down right under the post-mounted feeder," reported S.K. Kent, West Caldwell, New Jersey, in *Birds & Blooms*. "Since no squirrel has successfully reached the feeder, they don't even try to climb the pole anymore," he said.

"I call it a mobile feeder because I can place it anywhere I want. I used a threaded pipe for the post, which attaches to a 4-inch-diameter flange that sits in the bottom of a large ceramic flowerpot filled with concrete. It really works," he said.

## SQUIRREL-PROOF BIRD FEEDERS

Bird feeder designs have made great leaps toward being squirrel-proof. One of the first squirrel-proofs was the Hylarious feeder, which was built of steel and had weighted perches that allowed only lightweight birds to feed. When a squirrel or heavy bird sat on the perch to eat, its weight caused the perch bar to drop and seal off the seed supply. The perch weight was adjustable so that the owner could determine at what weight a bird or animal would be restricted from eating. This design and many

Droll Yankee's Jagunda Feeder

Homestead's Ultimate Stop-A-Squirrel bird feeder

like it that followed, work most of the time on squirrels and large, heavy birds. One exception appeared on a television show filmed in England, where two squirrels worked together, one squirrel sitting on the counterweight while the other squirrel ate the food.

Homestead's Ultimate Stop-A-Squirrel bird feeder has a weighted perch bar, too, but it also has a steep, smooth, powder-coated finish on the roof and sides that causes squirrels to slide off.

### Homemade Feeder

❀ Phyllis Sharpe of Ocala, Florida, baffled the squirrels from her bird feeders 10 years ago and hasn't had a violation since. According to her report in *Birder's World*, here's how she did it: "First, we chose a spot far enough away from trees or the roof to eliminate squirrels from jumping on top of the feeder. If they did, however, the metal surface with steep sides of our hand-made feeder would likely overwhelm them," she said. "The feeder has a detachable roof that lifts off to put in the seed. A baffle is placed under the feeder, outwitting even the most persistent squirrels. The sides of the roof overhang to such an extent that even unwanted crows cannot fit on the platform," she explained.

## CAGE THEM OUT

If you are handy, you can build an enclosure around any of your bird feeders to keep squirrels and other pests from getting to the birdseed. Make it with regular or plastic-coated hardware cloth or with chicken wire that has holes large enough to allow small birds to enter but with openings small enough to exclude squirrels and large birds. If you are not handy, stop in at your local wild-bird store, hardware store, or lawn-and-garden center, where you will find an assortment of ready-made enclosed bird feeders for sale.

Duncraft offers a variety of factory-made bird feeders that are caged in. The tray feeders and tube feeders are surrounded with green laminated mesh that allows chickadees, finches, nuthatches, juncos and other small birds to

This platform feeder made by Duncraft allows small birds in while excluding squirrels and larger birds.

The cage around this tube feeder keeps out unwanted guests while allowing songbirds such as goldfinches and chickadees to come and go.

feed inside while squirrels and larger bully birds are kept outside.

Droll Yankee has metal bands around some of its tube feeders, and metal feeding ports on others to prevent squirrels from chewing through the feeders. In addition, the company has tray feeders on posts that are equipped with baffles on top and bottom. Droll Yankee now offers a series of caged feeders as well that incorporate laminated mesh topped with a dome and fitted with a seed tray that also acts as a baffle.

❀ "I bought a feeder with a green metal cage around it from a local garden center," related Sue Narkiewicz of Albany. "I also switched to safflower seed. I heard that squirrels don't like that kind of seed," she explained. "Whatever the reason, the squirrels have disappeared."

### Cage Yourself In

❀ A gardener in Virginia built a huge chicken-wire house, tall enough to stand in, so that she could grow tomatoes without losing every one of them to the squirrels. It was extreme, but it worked.

## GIVE THEM THE SLIP

The invention of PVC pipes for plumbing had an effect on squirrels when it was discovered that squirrels can't climb them. Used as the post on which a bird feeder is mounted, it makes it impossible for squirrels to get any traction. One creative backyard birder decorated the PVC posts holding his bird feeder with white and black paint to make them look like white birch posts. He then drilled holes in the tops to wire the feeders in place.

This PVC post is painted to look like a white birch post.

❀ After setting a feeder post in the ground well away from trees and other objects from which squirrels could jump, Esther Ford, Bremen, Georgia, told *Bird Watcher's Digest* that she cut a four-inch diameter PVC pipe the same length as the post for her bird feeder, placed the PVC over the feeder post and erected the feeder. She found that the ground-to-feeder PVC works well to keep squirrels off the feeder.

### Greased Poles Work, Too

❀ "Try placing your feeder at least 8 feet from the nearest squirrel launching pad on a pole greased with Vaseline," recommend S. W. Lindley, of Cleveland, Ohio.

❀ "If anyone has a pole feeder and squirrel problem, here's a quick fix, claims Art Kramer of Southington,

Connecticut. "I spread shortening on the metal pole, starting at the top and spreading it down two feet. The squirrels go up and jump right off it. It works in the cold weather, too," he said.

## STRING A LINE OF OBSTACLES

Many people who had squirrel problems solved them by stringing a wire across the yard and then hanging their feeders from the wire. However, nearly everyone who has tried this has found that squirrels are quite adept at walking the high wire. That revelation has prompted the stringing of various articles on the wire to act as obstacles over which the squirrels cannot walk or jump to get to the feeders.

### Plastic Pop Bottles

❀ Carl Raduege of Waukesha got fed up with the squirrels raiding his bird feeders, too, and created his own devices to stop them. "In the bottom of a few plastic, two-liter juice bottles, I made a hole large enough to get around the post of my bird feeders. Then I slid a couple of them up the bird feeder post, one right behind the other, with the pole passing through the neck of the bottles to the feeder. I secured the bottles a few inches below the feeder by taping the neck of the bottle to the pole with duct tape." Carl used the same devices on a hanging feeder, sliding the bottles down the wire to position them above the feeder.

With the plastic bottles, Carl had devised a simple and inexpensive way to keep squirrels off his feeder. "They're still welcome to tidy up the seed that drops to the ground," Carl concedes.

❀ Peter C. Weber of Olney, Illinois, told *Birder's World* of his elaborate strategy: "My *almost* squirrel-proof feeder

Most squirrels can easily scramble along a clothesline or wire, but stringing plastic bottles along the route will deter them.

is a custom-made feeding station that supports one platform feeder and two tube feeders. All three were hung by pulleys and snapped to a 40-foot length of plastic-coated clothesline. One end of the wire is attached to a tree, the other to the house's deck with a turnbuckle and four large trampoline springs. The feeders can be pulled up to the house for filling. Then, a counterweight hung from a fixed pulley on the clothesline pulls the feeders back to the center of the yard.

"This setup alone foiled the squirrels for about a month, then they began walking along the clothesline to jump onto the feeders. My next step was to add plastic pop bottles. A hole was punched through the bottom center of each bottle so it could be threaded onto the clothesline. This deterred the squirrels from walking on the wire.

"However, one very acrobatic gray squirrel was able to skip nimbly along the top of the rolling bottles to get to the seed. So one more addition was made as I mounted an LP record to the wire. This has been greatly successful,"

Peter said. "Eventually, I'm sure the squirrels will learn to get around my safeguards, but it's been fun trying to foil the rascals."

❀ Plastic pop bottles strung on picture-hanger wire worked for Paul Benzer of Chippaqua, New York. He said he outwitted the squirrels with the bottles strung between ¾-inch galvanized electrical conduit (thin-walled pipe that can be bought at a hardware stores). "The number of bottles and length of conduit and picture-hanger wire you need depends on how long you want your squirrel spoofer to be," he explained in *Birds & Blooms*. "Mine was 18 feet long from the corner of my house to a pipe I planted in the yard. I drilled a hole just slightly larger than the picture-hanger wire through the caps and the bottoms of the bottles. I cut the conduit in 4-inch sections and then strung the bottles alternated with sections of conduit on the 18-foot long picture-hanging wire, like a necklace. I hung the squirrel spoofer at least 5 feet off the ground and at least 8 feet from the nearest tree. I placed at least three bottles on either side of the feeder. I promise you it works," he claims. "I've seen squirrels try to scamper across the bottles and conduit. They tumble off because the bottles spin so quickly," he said.

## OFFEND THEIR TASTE

### Hot Pepper

It was fashionable a few years ago to mix hot pepper powders—capsicum, cayenne, black pepper—with birdseed mix to keep squirrels from eating the seed. It works sometimes, but at other times the squirrels eat the seed regardless of how much pepper is added. An explanation for this inconsistent effectiveness comes from Dr. Larry Clark,

## FOODS SQUIRRELS DON'T LOVE

- **Niger (thistle) seed**
- **Suet without added ingredients**
- **Safflower seed**

head of repellent research at the National Wildlife Research Center, Fort Collins, Colorado, in *Gardening How-To* magazine: "All mammals, including squirrels, are irritated by the substance in black pepper and hot peppers. But it's the low-end gradient toward pain. So you have to ask yourself, 'What's the motivation status of the animal?' In other words, how hungry are those squirrels? In winter and spring, when other foods are scarce, birdseed and plant bulbs may be the most nutritious food the squirrels can find, so they'll put up with fiery paws and mouths to get them," he said.

Dr. Clark said that hot pepper deterrents are most likely to work in the summer, when squirrels can find plenty of other things to eat. The squirrels in my backyard, however, seem to have developed a fondness for the hot stuff regardless of the season, because they relished capsicum-coated seed even in the midst of summer.

### Switch to Safflower

Though squirrels are fond of almost everything that is offered in bird feeders, there are a couple of bird foods they don't like. Safflower seeds, the small, white, football-shaped seeds, are loved by most backyard birds, particularly cardinals, but not by squirrels. Safflower can be offered in the same feeders that are designed for sunflower seeds. Another food that squirrels don't relish is the tiny black niger (thistle) seed, a finch food that is offered in special tube feeders with tiny ports. Finches are crazy about niger, but squirrels aren't. And finally, plain white suet is a favorite of woodpeckers, chickadees and many other feeder birds, but not gray squirrels. If the suet cake has other ingredients, such as seed, insects, fruits or peanut butter mixed in, the gray squirrels will eat it, but not plain white suet.

❀ Like a growing number of backyard birders, Marcella Wolfert of Omaha, Nebraska, has switched from sunflower seeds to safflower seeds in her bird feeders. She told the readers of *Birds & Blooms* that the change in diet is popular with cardinals, house finches, chickadees, nuthatches and mourning doves, but the squirrels have turned down the new food.

## THE ODOR OFFENSIVE

Some people have been successful in deterring squirrels and other pests from their gardens with various scents.

### Hair

❀ "I couldn't tell you how many people have come into the shop in the last 16 years and asked for a bag of fresh hair clippings," said hairdresser Judi Jones of Detroit. "They swear that if you place it around vegetable gardens, the human smell will keep rabbits and squirrels and other animals out. Some people prefer to stuff the hair into old pantyhose and lay them about so that the hair doesn't blow away," she explained.

### Mothballs

❀ Harriet Walton of Tampa fills old nylon stockings with eight or so mothballs and hangs them near her feeding station to discourage squirrels. From time to time, she adds more mothballs to keep the scent strong. She reports that since she started doing this, she has just as many birds as ever—and no squirrels.

## Dried Blood

❀ Dried blood applied to bird feeders is recommended by the American Bird Society as a deterrent to squirrels. The only drawback to using this widely known soil conditioner, says the Society, is that you have to reapply it after each rain.

## Scent Masking

❀ To protect newly planted tulip, daffodil and other flower bulbs from being dug up and stolen by squirrels, a Michigan gardener suggests putting a few bulbs into a bag along with some cornstarch or talcum powder, which is supposed to disguise the smell of the bulbs. Shake the bag gently until the bulbs are completely coated with the powder. After the bulbs are planted, extra cornstarch can be sprinkled on top of the soil.

## TRAP THEM

When all else fails to keep the squirrels off the feeders, some people believe the ultimate solution may be to trap them and remove them from the area. One backyard bird watcher expressed it this way: "We consider the squirrels weeds in our garden and we merely remove them."

The most humane way to trap gray squirrels is in a live trap, such as a Havahart, with doors that fall when the squirrel touches the baited treadle. The most important part of the trapping process is to transport the prisoner as many miles away as possible so that it cannot return to the scene of the crime

This process works well enough if there are only one

A Havahart™ live trap allows you to remove unwanted visitors without harming them. (Photographed at Mitchell Park Horticultural Conservatory, Milwaukee, Wisconsin.)

or two squirrels in the neighborhood. Often, however, there are enough squirrels in the area so that as soon as one is removed, another moves in to take its place. A backyard birder in Cedarburg, Wisconsin, trapped and transported 49 gray squirrels out of his yard in one year but wound up with just as many as when he started.

Squirrels are protected by law in most states and inquiries should be made with the state wildlife agency before trapping and transporting squirrels.

## LEARN TO LIVE WITH THEM

A great many people who feed birds are not willing to fight the war against squirrels. Some simply like having the squirrels around and don't mind the fact that they eat birdseed. Others just don't have the time or the energy to wage the war. For these, there is a simple solution for dealing with squirrels: Give them their own food in their own

feeding area. By placing the kinds of foods that squirrels like—nuts, dried ear corn and sunflower seeds—on the ground or on a tray, well away from the bird feeders, the squirrels are likely to be satisfied and leave the bird feeders alone.

### Feed Them

❀ After years of battling squirrels at their feeding station, trying nearly every type of feeder and seed, Eric and Ginny Patton of Boulder, Colorado, started feeding the squirrels with the cheapest birdseed they could find. They set up a separate feeding area for the squirrels on the ground some distance from the bird feeders. Much to their surprise and delight, the squirrels were content to abandon the bird feeders in favor of the new setup. They spend only a few dollars a month on feeding the squirrels and have found that siskins, towhees and other birds are also attracted to the feeding area on the ground.

## The Nature of the Beast

Gray squirrels are large, slim, gray, tree-climbing rodents measuring 18 to 20 inches in length, half of which is the bushy tail. Adults weigh one to one-and-a-half pounds.

Surprisingly, gray squirrels come in a variety of shades and colors, from pure black to pure white and all shades of gray in between. Its expressive tail is a multipurpose tool that plays an important role in communication, locomotion and insulation. The tail is also a fifth leg, which helps maintain balance when the animal is on treetop excursions, performing tightrope acrobatics and chasing other squirrels.

Ideal gray squirrel habitat is a deciduous forest where oaks, beeches and hickories abound. This kind of wood-land provides gray squirrels with all the food and natural cover they need to prosper and raise young. They live in tree cavities in winter, often build leaf nests in summer and will readily use birdhouses. Their natural diet consists of nuts, fruits, berries, mushrooms and insects. Many subur-ban backyards offer similar natural habitat, with the added bonus of an abundance of bird food.

Gray squirrels are social animals. Each has a home range of less than an acre to more than 20 acres, which often overlaps with the home ranges of other gray squir-rels. Within the overlapping ranges, there is a well-defined social hierarchy. When squirrels meet—and they meet often—they recognize each other by sight and smell. This recognition includes the knowledge of which individual is dominant and which is subordinate.

Extremely vocal creatures, gray squirrels bark, chatter, scream, buzz, mew, purr and chuck. Further, the flashing and flickering movements of their eloquent tails, the stamping of their feet, the way they walk and the raising of the hairs on their bodies in conjunction with their vocalizations are all important components of squirrel communication.

Their long ears and large, dark eyes, located on the sides of their heads, are well suited for life in the trees. They also have a keen sense of smell, allowing them to find their cached food even when it's buried under several inches of snow and soil.

Two litters a year are the norm for gray squirrels, one in the winter and one in the summer. The winter solstice apparently triggers the primary mating season, when a

A baby squirrel peeks out of a house intended for birds.

female comes into heat and is pursued in a noisy, energetic chase through the treetops and up and down tree trunks by two to a dozen or more males.

About 44 days after being bred, the female gives birth to a litter of three to five tiny youngsters that are about 4½ inches long and weigh only ½ ounce. The helpless, naked and blind babies double in size in their first week on mother's milk. It takes another six weeks before the youngsters are developed enough to make their first wobbly forays outside the nest to feed on tender leaves. At 10 to 12 weeks, the young squirrels are weaned and are fending for themselves on a diet of solid foods. By then their mother may have bred again, following another chase through the treetops by a string of males.

As the summer passes, gray squirrels begin caching nuts in the ground as soon as there is a surplus. They will not dig them up until food is scarce again in the winter.

Do squirrels remember where they hide their nuts? Not very likely. They are more apt to find them, or the nuts buried by another squirrel, by scent.

Even under the best of circumstances, the average life span of a gray squirrel in the wild is only one year. About 25 percent of the population live longer, with a few living 12 or more years.

# RACCOONS

# The Problem with Raccoons

THE RACCOON IS A FOX in sheep's clothing when it comes to destroying other wildlife. Its engaging appearance and amusing behavior belie its role as the top predator of wildlife in North America, according to wildlife biologists. Every year, this masked bandit is responsible for the failure of millions of bird nests when it eats the eggs, young and often the parent birds sitting on the nests.

Raccoons are also at the top of the list of pests that destroy vegetable gardens. They are particularly fond of corn but are capable of eating an entire tomato or watermelon crop in one night.

In addition, raccoons are notorious for night raids at bird feeders, sometimes turning tube feeders upside-down to "drink" the seeds. They are leading destroyers of bird feeders, using their weight to pull them down and their teeth and feet to break them open.

Garbage cans, too, are favorite targets for raccoons in most of the country, especially those left at the curb for pickup. When they finish rummaging through the contents looking for morsels of discarded food, raccoons inevitably leave the open can tipped over, with the remaining trash strewn over a considerable area for the homeowner to deal with in the morning.

Some people make the mistake of falling for a raccoon's captivating, almost toylike appearance and its pathetic appeals for food. One clever raccoon being fed table scraps in Washington, D.C., lifted a door latch, walked into a kitchen, opened the refrigerator and helped

Entire families of raccoons will invade a backyard looking for birdseed and garbage. It is not a good idea to feed table scraps to these ring-tailed pilferers, as raccoons can carry rabies, roundworm, distemper, ringworm, mange and tuberculosis.

himself. In another incident involving people-friendly raccoons, a forest ranger claims to have seen a group of campers around a fire joined by raccoons that gradually edged closer to the circle until they were sitting with their hosts, enjoying the firelight and munching on hot dogs. That is a potentially dangerous event.

Raccoons are a primary carrier of rabies throughout North America. The transmission of the dangerous disease caused rabies epidemics among raccoons in the Northeast and the Mid-Atlantic states in the late 1980s. Many people have been bitten by raccoons in Georgia, Maryland, New Jersey, New York, Pennsylvania and Virginia, according to the Centers for Disease Control in Atlanta. For this reason alone, interaction with raccoons should be avoided, regardless of the circumstances.

Raccoons are also carriers of other diseases, including roundworm, canine distemper, ringworm, mange and tuberculosis. Any raccoon seen in daylight, acting strangely, boldly or aggressively is probably diseased and should be reported to the local authorities.

# War Stories

✳ Michael Baughman and his family were delighted when a family of black-capped chickadees moved into the little birdhouse they had hung from an apple tree in their suburban Chicago backyard. They watched excitedly as the sprightly pair carried moss, hair and fur into the little house in preparation for laying eggs. They observed the male chickadee bringing food to his mate while she sat on the eight eggs, and they knew when the babies hatched, because they saw both parents carry tiny morsels of food into the house. The feeding activity increased during the week after hatching and the chipping noises from inside the house grew louder with each passing day.

When the youngsters were nearing the time when they would leave the house, a tragedy struck. Early in the morning, Michael found the birdhouse on the ground with the roof torn off and corpses of baby chickadees in various stages of mutilation scattered on the ground. Scratches on the house and the ferocity with which the structure had been torn from the tree and ripped apart were evidence of the work of one or more raccoons. "It was a devastating sight," said Michael.

✳ A.B.C. Whipple of Greenwich, Connecticut, who had been engaged in combat with raccoons for years, reported that the raccoons distributed his garbage along the driveway, arranged into dinner courses. Whipple once related in *Reader's Digest* how he heard the clanging of the garbage can

Garbage cans are a favorite target for clever and adroit raccoons to raid.

lid one night. Investigating, he found the lid closed but could hear unmistakable shuffling noises within the can. As he approached, the top opened, lifted by the head of a large raccoon that nimbly climbed out, glanced in Whipple's direction with what he took to be a look of gratitude and sauntered away. In hindsight, Whipple realizes that it was the look of benign contempt.

Raccoons are leading destroyers of bird feeders, using their weight to pull them down and their teeth and feet to break them open.

✳ A woman in Scarsdale, New York, reported in the *New York Times* that when she stored her garbage in the garage to keep the raccoons from getting it, the raccoons ate their way through the garage roof.

✳ Raccoons found a veritable banquet in the backyard of the Holmeses in Pine Grove Mills, Pennsylvania, where the family had fed birds for years. Except for an occasional gray squirrel in the area, there had been no significant problems with pests getting the food until one July morning when all of their bird feeders were on the ground and empty. The feeders were replaced to their original hanging and post positions where the birds could use them again and it was hoped that the night raid was a one-time affair. Not surprisingly, it was not. The following morning the feeders were again in disarray and this time several were damaged.

The next night, the Holmeses stayed up to wait for the night raiders to strike. The ring-tailed pilferers arrived at about 10:30 and immediately went about their business. After turning on a yard light, the Holmeses watched in amazement as an entire family of raccoons—a mother and five cubs—meticulously and dexterously pulled down all the feeders and devoured the contents.

✳ Shirley Most of Sioux Falls was surprised but delighted to see a handsome raccoon in the beam of her patio spotlight. The winsome animal was having a meal of seed from her bird feeder. Excited, Shirley got some leftover bread and cake from the kitchen and tossed it out the door to the raccoon. Sure enough, the coon scarfed up the offerings and waited for more.

Before dark the following night, Shirley put out table scraps in anticipation of her previous night's visitor. She didn't have to wait long. The big raccoon appeared as expected, but this time it brought the rest of the family. Shirley was thrilled to see the mother raccoon with her four babies, all eating table scraps with their deft hands. They even carried some of the bread to the birdbath, dipped it into the water and then ate it. The nightly visits continued through the late summer

Raccoons are notorious for night raids at bird feeders, sometimes turning tube feeders upside-down to "drink" the seeds.

and into the fall. The number of customers increased from the original family of six to several families, at times totaling 16 animals. It was a nightly animal circus, all happening on Shirley's patio. What fun!

The fun ended when Shirley took a two-week vacation trip, leaving the raccoons to fend for themselves. When she got home, she was horrified to find that all of her bird feeders had been knocked down and destroyed, the garden looked like a war zone and the patio windows and door were seriously damaged with claw and chew marks. The raccoons were not to be denied their food.

Shirley was so upset that she called the local game warden for help. She soon realized that she had created a huge problem that would end in the demise of the raccoons and a repair and replacement bill that was not in her budget.

✻ A licensed trapper trapped and removed more than 30 raccoons from one 50 x 20-foot suburban Milwaukee backyard. He said it wasn't unusual to trap large numbers of raccoons on small lots.

✻ A woman who petitioned the local village council for raccoon-control measures told officials that raccoons tore holes in the siding of one house, slid down the chimney and entered the living room of another and damaged rain gutters of still another. In the same village, a pair of raccoons moved into a house and lived there for about a year before being detected. "I didn't realize it until one of them came walking down the stairs at 1:00 a.m.," the homeowner said.

✻ Stan Schwartz of Indianapolis tended his garden of corn, tomatoes and squash daily. One morning in August, when the vegetables were just about ripe, he awakened to find his garden in a shambles. "It was like a tractor had gone through it," he said. The corn stalks were on the ground, with the ears torn off and half eaten. The tomatoes were off the vines and smashed. The squash was a

Raiding backyard vegetable gardens is also a favorite pastime of raccoons. They are particularly fond of corn but are capable of decimating an entire tomato or watermelon crop in one night.

mess. Tracks in the soil told the story. A family of raccoons had helped themselves to Stan's vegetable garden, leaving nothing for him.

## Solutions

The best way to deal with raccoons is to deny them food and denning sites. That means removing or restricting their access to bird feeders, much like foiling squirrels. Large, sturdy baffles on post feeders and domes over the tops of hanging feeders will usually keep raccoons from reaching the bird food.

Raccoons that visit garbage cans can be stopped with raccoon-proof cans, which have lids that cannot be removed by these clever and adroit looters. In addition, by sealing off or restricting entrances to homes and outbuildings, including chimneys, raccoons will not be able to nest or den there. In other words, if there are no food sources or denning sites available, raccoons will have to move elsewhere to find these amenities.

## CHIMNEY DWELLERS

Raccoons that have already taken up residence in attics and chimneys have to be removed.

On arriving home from a trip abroad in early May, I heard strange noises coming from inside the fireplace. On closer examination, there were foul odors, too.

By opening the damper, I could see and hear baby raccoons just above the damper at the bottom of the chimney. After a great deal of hard work dismantling the damper, I put on a pair of heavy leather gloves and was able to reach up into the chimney and pick up the babies one at a time and remove them. A wire screen cover was installed on top of the chimney to keep the absent mother from reentering.

Some people with this same problem have banished raccoons from the chimney with loud noises, such as a blaring boom box playing hard rock music. It worked for a Nebraska family who had a nest of raccoons in their fireplace chimney. After a few hours of boom box music, the mother raccoon was seen removing one cub at a time from the chimney to a new nest site in the neighbor's yard. A barking dog has been effective in some cases.

Others have wisely called upon the services of companies that specialize in removing pest animals like raccoons from people's attics, garages and chimneys (in the Yellow Pages under *Animal Removal Services* or *Pest Control Services*). One company in New York, responding to such a request, arrived on the scene in outfits that looked like those in *Ghostbusters*, including heavy gloves, nets and ladders.

Local wildlife agencies or wildlife rehabilitation centers may also respond to some requests for removal of raccoons. Others merely offer the use of a live trap that must be tended by the homeowner.

> **Don't be deceived by the raccoon's cuddly appearance; they can be very dangerous animals and extreme care and wariness should be used in any dealings with them. Unless they are small, helpless babies and you are wearing impenetrable leather gloves to protect your hands from bites, never attempt to handle a raccoon yourself.**

## TRAPPING AND TRANSPORTING RACCOONS

Raccoons may be attracted by live traps baited with sardines, but because of their high intellect, they may be wary of traps. Should a raccoon be trapped once and survive the experience, that individual will probably never be trapped again. A trapped raccoon should be transported a long way from home, at least five miles, so that it doesn't return to the scene of its crime spree.

Raccoons are protected by law in many states and inquiries should be made with the state wildlife agency before trapping and transporting raccoons.

## THE GARDEN CHALLENGE

To keep raccoons out of gardens, a strong and sturdy fence may not be enough. Raccoons are good climbers and can scale most fences. However, if the fence is augmented by a charged electric wire that shocks anything it touches, raccoons will get the message.

A predator guard such as this one will keep nesting birds out of the reach of raccoons.

To keep raccoons from destroying the contents of birdhouses, secure the house firmly to the post or tree on which it is mounted. The same goes for the lid of the house, so that a raccoon cannot pry it off with its dexterous hands. Raccoons will prey on wood ducks nesting in birdhouses if they can remove the lids or get their hands and arms far enough through the entrance holes to reach the sitting hen. A predator guard mounted on the outside of the entrance hole of any birdhouse should keep raccoons and other four-legged, tree-climbing predators from reaching in far enough to grab the hen, chicks or eggs.

# The Nature of the Beast

Raccoons are common throughout North America, except in very high mountains, the arctic and desert regions. They prefer farmlands, woods, parks, cities and suburban back-yards near water.

An adult raccoon may measure 20 to 30 inches long from nose to tail and weigh from 10 to 35 pounds. Males are larger and heavier than females. One monster in Wisconsin weighed 62 pounds and measured 4 feet, 7 inches from nose to tail. Southern raccoons are smaller than those in the North. In the Florida Keys, adult raccoons may weigh as little as four or five pounds.

Because raccoons are nocturnal, nearly all of the damage they cause is perpetrated at night.

Raccoons are somewhat sociable, particularly during breeding seasons and they may den with other raccoons during the cold winter months. Yet, raccoons aren't true hibernators. They are inactive during most of the winter, sleeping for days or weeks at a time but do not shut down completely like some animals do during winter. An ideal den site is a cavity in a large tree, although raccoons will also use manmade structures such as attics, chimneys and outbuildings.

Beginning in January, while the females are still in their dens, male raccoons become active. They travel about looking for mates, checking every spot that might harbor a female. When a male finds a female, she may or may not

A raccoon's den site is, ideally, in a large tree cavity, but they will also use manmade structures such as attics, chimneys and outbuildings.

A raccoon's forepaws are almost as nimble as those of a monkey, enabling it to climb trees, open doors, unscrew jar lids, uncork bottles and lift latches

accept him. If she does, the male moves into her den for a week or two of courtship and breeding before moving on to look for another mate.

The female, having been bred, goes back to sleep to wait for spring. Her kits, usually four, will be born during April or May. The three-ounce furry babies are blind and helpless at birth but grow quickly. Their eyes open when they are about three weeks old and when they are 10 weeks old they start to accompany their mothers on nightly forays, learning how to pick berries, catch crayfish, raid bird feeders and open garbage cans. The youngsters stay in the tutelage of their mothers until late fall and then the family splits up, each to find its own hollow tree or burrow for the winter.

Omnivorous, the raccoon will consume nearly anything, including aquatic animals, fruits, nuts, cultivated grains, birdseed, bird eggs, small mammals, birds and garbage. Feats like opening eggs are possible because of the raccoon's amazing dexterity. Its forepaws are almost as nimble as those of a monkey. It can effortlessly open doors, unscrew jar lids, uncork bottles and lift latches.

Anyone who has had a family of raccoons nesting in their chimney or in a tree at the back door knows that they communicate with a variety of whimpers, whines, squeals, screams, churrs, purrs and chitters.

Average longevity for an adult raccoon is about six years in the wild, but 10 to 14 years in captivity.

# HOUSE CATS

# The Problem with House Cats

EVERY DAY IN MILLIONS of backyards, house cats crouch in ambush under bird feeders, waiting for the right moment to catch songbirds. Many of those house cats are successful.

According to *FeederWatch News*, a quarterly newsletter from the Cornell Laboratory of Ornithology, cats were second only to sharp-shinned hawks as the most frequent predators at bird feeders in the United States and Canada.

People who own pet cats that are permitted to run freely outdoors usually are reluctant to hear that house cats are among the world's greatest predators of wildlife. "Not my cat," is the usual retort. "She gets all the food she can eat at home."

Yet recent studies in the United States and Great Britain dramatically confirm that house cats, including those that are well fed at home, are responsible for the deaths of many millions of small birds every year, a death toll that may be contributing to declines in some rare species.

"The fact that they [the cats] had been fed already and were not particularly hungry made no difference to the number of prey they killed each day, because the urge to hunt is independent of the urge to eat," explained animal behavior expert Desmond Morris, author of *Catwatching*. "Cats hunt for the sake of hunting," he concluded.

"It's shocking," said Dr. Stanley Temple, professor of Wildlife Ecology and Conservation at the University of Wisconsin, Madison. Temple and colleague John Coleman

The benign, cuddly house cat becomes a lethal predator when allowed to prowl outdoors. One study in Wisconsin showed that in that state alone, cats kill at least 19 million songbirds and 140,000 game birds annually.

completed a four-year study on the impact of free-ranging domestic cats on rural wildlife. By radio-collaring many farm cats for various periods of time, the researchers found that in Wisconsin alone, cats kill at least 19 million song-birds and 140,000 game birds annually.

The Wisconsin findings followed a British study that shocked cat lovers around the world when biologists Peter Church and John Lawton published their data about the predatory habits of 78 house cats living in Church's home village in Bedfordshire, England.

Because house cats typically bring home about 50 per-cent of the prey they kill and present their "trophies" to their owners, Church enlisted the cooperation of 77 of the 78 cat owners in his village to gather their cats' grizzly offerings into poly bags and save them for the scientists.

Based on the astonishing collection of bones, feathers and fur collected in just one village in one year, Church and Lawton estimated that Britain's 5 million house cats account for an annual toll of some 70 million animals, 20 million of which are birds.

These findings are disturbing to most cat owners, who do not want to feel responsible for the demise of neighborhood wildlife. The Wisconsin study found that 94 percent of cat owners said they wanted songbirds on their property and 83 percent wanted game birds, yet only 42 percent were willing to reduce the numbers of free-roaming cats to benefit these species.

"Cat owners demonstrate a lot of denial about the hunting achievements of their cats," Temple noted. "In fact, they seem to have a certain pride in their cats' prowess and believe it to be 'neat' that their kitty cats can kill wildlife," he remarked. "At the same time, they are convinced that their cats are harmless."

As one cat owner insisted, "My free-roaming cat rarely leaves our yard. Besides, cats prefer to eat rodents over birds and she keeps down the population of chipmunks and the rats that have invaded Atlanta."

Cats' innate hunting instinct, compounded by rapidly increasing numbers of free-roaming and feral cats in the U.S., is causing a wildlife problem of enormous proportions, a problem that has wildlife managers scratching their heads.

# War Stories

 "It seems as if my beginner's luck is over," reported a backyard bird watcher on the Internet. "I now have two cats that are stalking my yard and feeders. I have baffles on my feeders; however, I have feeder arms hanging out from my deck and one cat is so brazen that it comes and sits on my deck in the morning and has driven my birds away. I

According to FeederWatch News, cats are second only to sharp-shinned hawks as the most frequent predators at bird feeders in the United States and Canada.

have bluebirds in a nesting box and I want to get these cats off my property. I don't know who they belong to."

🦋 "I have an indoor cat, but a neighbor's cat keeps coming on our deck bothering both the birds and my indoor cat," claimed another backyard birder.

🦋 Bob and Nancy Barton's adopted streetwise stray, Alley, has upset his chosen humans on a number of occasions with his highly honed bird hunting skills. In their Houston, Texas, backyard, Alley has not only presented the Bartons with songbird remains on a fairly regular basis, but has horrified them with his major league batting skills. He has become quite adept at swatting down hummingbirds with his paws as they near flowers in the lush backyard.

# Solutions

## THE BEST SOLUTION: CONFINE CATS

The best and easiest way to end the destruction of wildlife by free-roaming pet house cats is for owners to keep their cats indoors. This control measure also protects the pets from being killed or harmed by other animals, vehicles and diseases.

However, most cat owners aren't convinced. "Oh, I couldn't keep my cat inside all the time. I have to let her out, at least for a little while, or she would go crazy," many claim.

That's nonsense, of course. While cats hate any change in their usual routines, they do adapt and they are just as comfortable and stand a better chance of living a healthier, happier, longer life in one-room apartments as on 100-acre farms. True, you and your cat may have a battle of wills for a while over this new arrangement, but persistence on your part will pay off in the long run, resulting in a healthier and more companionable pet.

❀ "My cats used to free-roam because I, like so many people, thought a cat simply couldn't be happily contained," Jane Wille of Morgantown, North Carolina, told *Bird Watcher's Digest*. "But as one converted, I am writing to tell the nonbelievers that, indeed, cat containment is possible and, once adjusted to, extremely desirable."

❀ Indoor cats can be dedicated but harmless bird watchers if their owners create a backyard bird watching microcosm outside the windows of the house, with bird feeders, birdbaths and protective vegetation. (See *Bird Watching for Cats* by Kit and George Harrison, Willow Creek Press, 1998.)

## BELLS AND DECLAWING DON'T WORK

Bells and declawing don't work, according to Dr. Temple. "Wildlife does not associate the ringing of a bell with a predator. Besides, when cats stalk their prey their stealth makes them nearly motionless. The bell doesn't ring," he explained.

"Declawed cats don't stop hunting, either. Without claws, they simply bat down their prey," he said.

## WATER IS AN EFFECTIVE DETERRENT

❀ "I've read that you can train a cat to stay away from things with a squirt bottle or squirt pistol," reported a bird watcher on an Internet message board. "We had water pistols at the ready whenever our cat went near our gerbils. It didn't take long for the lesson to be learned."

❀ "I got a pot of water and threw it toward the cat that was on my deck and this seemed to keep the cat away without harming it," another said.

❀ "I agree with the water method," claimed one of several more. "If you can't get close to the cat, buy a large squirt gun that will reach a long distance and soak the cat every time it enters your yard. If it gets on your deck, soak it there also. Even pouring water on it is not cruel as long as the water is cool."

## TRAPPING CATS FOR THE HUMANE SOCIETY

Free-roaming cats that have no apparent owner can be live-trapped and taken to the local Humane Society. A large live trap, such as one made by Havahart, baited with

Most cat owners do not want to feel responsible for the demise of neighborhood wildlife, yet only 42 percent were willing to reduce the numbers of free-roaming cats to benefit game and songbird populations.

canned fish and placed under natural cover, should catch the culprits. (Be prepared to capture raccoons, skunks and opossums as well.) Use care in transporting a prisoner, as some feral cats are quite wild and can be dangerous, or may even be diseased.

❀ "My husband borrowed a trap for cats from a friend who works at the local Humane Society," a backyard bird watcher related. "The cats he catches are not injured and he just carries them to the Humane Society where they are taken care of."

## NEUTERING

According to the Humane Society of the United States, one female cat and her offspring can produce a staggering 420,000 cats in just seven years. Though this figure is based on the cats reproducing at maximum capacity, even half that number is reason enough to have your pet neutered. Obviously, the countryside is already overrun with free-roaming cats and it's time to accept the idea of neutering to reduce their reproductive capacity and to give wildlife a break. An additional bonus to you is that, statistically, your pet has a better chance of living longer. A neutered tomcat, for example, averages three more years of life than one who has not been altered, mostly because they are far less prone to getting into fights with other cats and for some reason, are less susceptible to infection.

## The Nature of the Beast

Though the Egyptians took the first cats as house pets some 3,500 years ago, domestic cats are still not far removed from their wild relatives. A *National Geographic* television special, "Cat: Caressing the Tiger," showed graphic footage of how the behavior of an eight-pound house cat often resembles that of a 600-pound tiger. One minute it is a purring ball of fur in its owner's lap; the next, it is a wild animal possessing the ruthless killing instincts of a lion on the Serengeti.

"Once a cat leaves the front door it assumes the temperament of a wild animal with a singular line of work—to kill efficiently," the documentary dramatized.

It also featured another English study of cats by Oxford's David Macdonald, who discovered that a population of 80 farm cats in a barnyard north of London lived together in social hierarchies surprisingly like those of lion prides. Like lions, related females, such as aunts, cousins, grandmothers and daughters, nursed one another's young. Also like lions, males killed whole litters of kittens so that females would come into heat sooner and produce litters sired by them.

*Felis catus* is prolific, capable of breeding two to three times a year and producing litters averaging four kittens. The kittens are born blind and helpless, but on a diet of mother's milk they are quite active in four to six weeks, rolling and playing with each other and exploring the world around them. They are weaned in eight weeks and, depending on nutrition and general health, females are capable of breeding in seven to twelve months, although a few come into estrus as young as four months of age. Males generally reach puberty at about nine months.

House cats live very well on a diet of commercial cat foods while those that are free-ranging may supplement their diets with small mammals, birds, insects and fish.

Free-ranging house cats might live eight to ten years, while those kept at home can enjoy the good life for up to 16 or even 20 or more years.

The best and easiest way to end the destruction of wildlife by free-roaming house cats is for owners to keep their cats indoors.

# DEER

# The Problem with Deer

IN FORESTS, ON FARMLANDS and in suburban America,
exploding white-tailed deer populations are wreaking
havoc by eating virtually everything green. In some urban
and suburban areas, the deer have become as pesky as city
pigeons and as dangerous as drunken drivers.

Among the 13 states with the highest whitetail populations, deer numbers have surged an average of 42 percent
in the last decade. In Georgia alone, the sixth most popu-
lated whitetail state, deer numbers soared 134 percent
since the mid-1980s; 78 percent in Missouri; 70 percent in
Virginia; and 69 percent in Michigan.

It is estimated that the total population for 43 states
where white-tailed deer live has risen above 25 million for
the first time since European settlers arrived. According to
wildlife biologists, deer populations exploded during the
1980s and 1990s for a variety of reasons.

Unseasonably warm winters throughout North America
during the past 15 years have given deer an unnaturally
high winter survival rate, particularly among yearling deer.

Traditional conservative hunting seasons and bag limits have continued while deer populations expanded.
Bucks-only traditions are so deeply ingrained in so many
deer hunters that they balk at shooting deer without
antlers, even when it's allowed. In addition, posted lands
and lands leased to hunting clubs have protected deer from
public hunting.

Agricultural and timber production have increased
with the use of more effective fertilizers and mechanized

equipment, providing more and better food and habitat for deer.

Deer habitat has also improved in suburbs as real estate planners and backyard wildlife landscapers have designed properties with habitats for birds that are also perfect for white-tailed deer, complete with optimum food (shrubs, flowers and birdseed), water and cover. At first, many suburbanites love having deer around their homes and they often feed them. But when deer multiply and eat everything in the backyard that is green, attitudes change. Without the control that hunting provides, deer numbers in urban and suburban areas grow unabated.

# War Stories

✳ One fall, the birds in the backyard of Pam Painter of Poseyville, Indiana, appeared to develop an appetite for midnight snacks. According to a report in *Birds & Blooms*, three feeders would be completely emptied every night. After hearing animals wandering around in the yard, Pam's mother became suspicious and was convinced that deer were eating the birdseed. That sounded strange to Pam, because their house is located in the heart of town, surrounded by neighbors and a hospital. She kidded her mother about the deer theory. But one snowy morning, Pam had to capitulate when her mother spotted hoof prints around the bird feeders. Since then, Pam and her mother have seen deer as often as they see birds at the feeders.

✳ A 43-year-old woman and her female companion were driving on Highway M57 in Saginaw County, Michigan, at 9:00 p.m. on a dark, dry, clear November night. When a deer appeared on the road ahead, the woman swerved the

Exploding deer populations are wreaking havoc in America's backyards. Deer eat virtually everything that's green.

car, lost control, struck a ditch and rolled over. Both women were killed.

❧ After a deer crashed through a window at Jordan's Gift Shop in Princeton, New Jersey, in September, the community had enough. A new ordinance was passed to allow shotgun hunting in the city limits for the first time since 1972 to control the deer that were mangling shrubbery, crushing flower beds and causing nearly 200 vehicle accidents a year.

❧ In Bloomington, Minnesota, a woman presented a garbage can full of deer droppings from her backyard to the city council while they were debating what to do about the city's deer problem. The plan that followed called for

Backyard habitats for birds are also perfect for whitetails, complete with optimum food (shrubs, flowers and birdseed), water and cover.

police sharp-shooters to kill several hundred deer within the city limits. Though hundreds have now been removed, there are still too many deer in the city.

❋ Tick checks are a nightly routine for seven-year-old James Cassell and his five-year-old sister Katherine, who live with their parents in northern Westchester County, New York. The ticks are carried by the many deer that daily parade through the Cassells' backyard. Two summers ago, a tick bite on James' ear became red and inflamed, prompting a five-week treatment for Lyme disease. After losing four pounds and sleeping 16 hours a day for several weeks, the young boy recovered.

❋ Looking out the window of their farmhouse in rural Mississippi, the Brown family counted close to 200 whitetailed deer in their soybean field. They have permits to shoot the deer, but hunting down that many deer would be a full-time, if not impossible, job.

# Solutions

## HUNTING

There is only one practical, acceptable, effective way to reduce or control a population of deer and that is by public hunting. However, when the deer are in urban settings, public hunting may be unsafe, illegal or impractical. For those reasons, communities throughout the country continue to grapple with the controversial subject of how to reduce deer numbers within a metropolitan district.

The most popular alternative to hunting is to trap the deer and transport them out of the area. Yet trapping is costly, slow, and some deer have returned to their original home range after release in the wild, even from great distances.

The hiring of sharpshooters has also been employed extensively. Though this method has been more successful than trapping, it has also been more controversial.

If you live in the country and have the space, putting out a salt-lick will attract deer to within viewing distance of your house. When they arrive, however, they may also eat your shrubs and flowers.

Deer contraceptives have been tried as well, but they are so impractical and difficult to administer that they have been ineffectual.

The search continues for the perfect, most acceptable and most effective control of urban deer populations. Meanwhile, their numbers continue to rise.

## EXCLOSURES

On smaller tracts, such as a backyard garden or an orchard, the most effective, foolproof method for keeping out deer is a fence. Because deer are expert jumpers, the fence has to be at least eight feet high and sturdy enough to keep the animals from breaking through it.

The best deer fence is one like this—a combination of a heavy wire fence, at least eight feet tall, with an electric strand on top.

Electric fencing, like that used to keep cattle in, is effective, too, but only if it has at least three strands, preferably four or five, all charged. To exclude deer, the animal must touch the electric wire and learn that it is unpleasant. The major drawback to electric fencing is that it requires constant maintenance to keep vegetation from grounding it.

The best deer fence is a combination of a heavy wire fence, eight feet tall or higher, with an electric strand on top. Such a fence is expensive, but if it promises to safeguard an orchard, the cost may be justified.

## SCREENING

Gardeners who cover plants with green plastic mesh over the winter have a chance of keeping deer from eating the plants, because deer do not like to stick their tongues through mesh.

By building strong screen houses over garden plots, or using row covers of plastic mesh or hardware cloth, garden plots can be deer-proofed. Upside-down plastic laundry baskets will protect individual plants as long as the baskets are held securely in place.

## REPELLENTS

There has been vast research devoted to developing deer repellents—mostly chemicals that are sprayed on plants to deter deer from eating them. According to one study, two of the three most effective repellents are foul smelling and the third has a bitter taste: Deer-Away, made from putrefied egg whites, cannot be used on food crops; Hinder is an ammonium soap; and bitter-tasting Thiram is used in some commercial repellents.

Other repellents that may work for a while, on at least some deer, include bar soaps such as Irish Spring, Dial, Safeguard and Ivory. Dissolve the soaps in water and spray them on the plants you are trying to protect, or sprinkle shavings on the plants. Some people hang bars of soap on the plants.

❀ Toni Fulco of East Stroudsburg, Pennsylvania, found that deer-proofing a flower bed or favorite shrubs can be done economically by tying bars of perfumed soap to the shrubs, trees or plants you want to protect. She told the readers of *Birds & Blooms* that she uses an ice pick to make a hole in the soap for twine and then ties the bars where needed. Other people put the soap in old nylon stockings and hang it in a tree. Toni hangs the soap high enough to keep it out of reach of the skunks and opossums that find it a tasty treat.

❀ A wildlife study in Washington showed that predator fecal odors were effective in repelling black-tailed deer. The feces of bobcats and mountain lions were the most effective.

Horticultural experts say that all deer repellents are subject to failure if the deer are hungry enough, as they may be in late winter when food is scarce. Deer will eat anything, even if it has repellent on it. Also, most repellents wash away in a rain, requiring frequent reapplications. Some, like soaps, have a very small radius of effectiveness, not more than 6 to 7 inches. Some other repellents are effective at a somewhat greater range.

Hanging bars of soap, such as Irish Spring, Dial or Safeguard, from trees or shrubs will often keep deer from eating them. You can also dissolve the soap in water and spray it on the plants you are trying to protect. (Photographed at Mitchell Park Horticultural Conservatory, Milwaukee, Wisconsin.)

# URINE LORE

Under the classification of "Old Wives' Tales" is the use of urine as a deterrent to deer. Yet there are people who swear by it. Those who have studied the subject claim that urine works best if it comes from a carnivore that has eaten meat in the hours prior to urinating. That includes humans.

❀ Jane read somewhere that human urine was an effective deer repellent. So she suggested to her husband, Jim, that they try it at their Land-O-Lakes, Wisconsin, home where the deer were raiding their garden. Jim began making nightly forays to the garden to relieve himself. Soon afterward, they had a house full of overnight guests, to whom Jane and Jim explained their deer-repellent program and asked the male visitors to participate. The men obliged by anointing assigned segments of the garden before going to bed. After several weeks of treatments by Jim and various guests, the couple noticed a lack of new deer damage to their garden. Because they knew that rain reduced the effectiveness of the urine, Jim continued to administer new applications and the deer continued to stay away.

❀ Alice and John, too, had heard that predator urine was an effective deer repellent, so Alice prevailed upon a zookeeper friend to procure some lion urine. They poured the lion urine onto blotter paper, which they then attached to the bottoms of tin cans that were hung from strings around their garden in Hazelhurst, Wisconsin. Lo and behold, the deer disappeared. The blotter papers were saturated with lion urine after every rain to keep them fresh and they continued to be effective for five years.

## SOUND REPELS

Deer don't like loud noises, so they can be kept out of gardens and away from bird feeders for a limited time by noises such as shellcrackers, propane exploders, cap guns and boom boxes. But these noises also repel birds and annoy nearby neighbors. Eventually the deer may become accustomed to the noise, rendering the tactic ineffective.

❀ Peggy Price of Elm Grove, Louisiana, says in *Birds & Blooms* that a clock radio in the garden, set for the music alarm to come on shortly after sunset, will keep deer away.

❀ In Philadelphia, gardeners were so desperate to repel deer that they tried hanging hubcaps in the wind where they banged against each other. It worked for a while.

This white-tailed deer is enjoying a breakfast of begonias in a Wisconsin backyard.

**PLANTS DEER DON'T LOVE**

| | |
|---|---|
| Ageratum | Scotch pine |
| Begonia | Mountain pine |
| Cleome | White spruce |
| Cornflower | Norway spruce |
| Dusty Miller | Rose-of-Sharon |
| Lobelia | Japanese cedar |
| Marigold | Flowering dogwood |
| Nicotiana | Fraser fir |
| Salvia | American holly |
| Pear | Common boxwood |

## DEER-RESISTANT PLANTS

Deer love hostas, geraniums and impatiens and many other flowers and shrubs. They also prefer fertilized plants over unfertilized plants. They do not like highly aromatic herbs, such as mint, lavender, sage, rosemary and thyme. Nor do they like leathery foliage, like holly, which also has thorns. Among some of the other plants that are deer-resistant and which would be good replacements for the plants deer have eaten, according to *Gardening How-To* magazine, are the following:

**Ageratum**: Blue or white flowers last all summer.
**Begonia**: Good choice for shade; many colors.
**Cleome**: "Spider flower" adds height with tall stems.
**Cornflower**: "Bachelor's button" will flower all summer.
**Dusty Miller**: Silvery foliage provides lovely contrasts.
**Lobelia**: Perfect edging plant; in blue, white or purple.
**Marigold**: Fiery colors; a classic in kitchen gardens.
**Nicotiana**: "Flowering tobacco;" many are fragrant.
**Salvia**: Comes in red, blue, purple and white.

In a study in Greenwich, Connecticut, deer did not eat

Among 13 states with the highest whitetail populations, deer numbers have surged an average of 42 percent in the last decade. One reason is that unseasonably warm winters throughout North America during the past 15 years have given deer an unnaturally high winter survival rate.

the following ornamental plants, according to a report in the *Wildlife Society Bulletin:* pear, Scotch pine, mountain pine, white spruce, Norway spruce, Rose-of-Sharon, Japanese cedar, flowering dogwood, Fraser fir, American holly and common boxwood.

# The Nature of the Beast

There are only two species of deer in North America: the white-tailed and the mule deer. They are members of a family of mammals known as *Cervidae.* In North America, that also includes moose, caribou and elk.

White-tailed deer are divided into 30 subspecies (including the diminutive Florida Key deer), which range widely throughout North America from near-arctic regions in Canada to the tropics in Mexico and into Central and South America.

Mule deer are classified into seven subspecies (including the Columbian and Sitka black-tailed deer) that range throughout western North America from Alaska to Mexico.

In summer, the whitetail's coat is reddish above with white on its face, throat and underbody; in winter, the animal is grayish-brown to nearly blue above. Compared to a whitetail, a mule deer has longer ears and more bounce to its gait.

Most white-tailed deer stand two and a half to three feet tall at the shoulder and are four to six feet long from their nose to the base of their tail. The average weight of an adult is 125 to 175 pounds, although some have weighed more than 400 pounds and at least two were over 500 pounds. Bucks are larger than does and, generally, the farther south a whitetail lives, the smaller its body size. A Florida Key deer, for example, stands only 28 inches high at the shoulder and weighs 35 to 80 pounds, about the size of a German shepherd. A whitetail living in the upper Midwest is two to three times larger.

The whitetail's principal field mark is its white tail, which is white only on the underside. The deer often raises its tail as a danger signal to alert other deer in the group so that they can flee in a unit.

The whitetail's white-flag alarm is often accompanied by a snort or "blow." It also communicates threats by stomping its front feet, which sometimes happens when a deer sees a person but isn't sure what it is looking at.

The white-tailed deer is a living fortress of sensory devices designed to protect itself against predators. Its ears are ever swinging this way and that, searching for sounds of danger with its acute hearing. If its keen sense of smell picks up a whiff of predator or human, the tail goes up and the deer is gone. Many backyard deer, however, become accustomed to human scent and grow comfortable entering a garden.

Before humans flooded the continent, white-tailed deer were mostly the prey of mountain lions and wolves. Today, free-running dogs inflict the highest predator toll, while man exercises the greatest control over deer numbers.

Deer are browsers and usually find an abundance of twigs and buds from deciduous plants and coniferous growth throughout the winter. They also graze on grasses, herbs, mushrooms, garden flowers and vegetables and, at times, they will grub for roots. They digest their food as ruminants, by chewing a cud and processing it through a four-compartment stomach.

Deer biologists estimate that natural reproduction accounts for a 20 to 30 percent increase in deer numbers at the end of each summer. This dramatic leap in the population is then reduced by natural mortality, hunting and accidents. In urban and suburban areas, where hunting is prohibited, deer populations are not reduced annually.

Both whitetails and mule deer are sexually active from October through December as the hours of daylight shorten. Buck deer are animals of opportunity and breed whatever does are available to them. A buck's normal home range may be an oval of two to three square miles, depending on topography, food and habitat. During the breeding season, his range may expand to ten to 12 square miles.

Does become fertile with the onset of estrus in October. They are receptive to the males for only a 24- to 30-hour period. If not impregnated, the doe's cycle is repeated at 28-day intervals at least three times, or until she is bred. The birth of fawns follows in about 201 days.

Among doe fawns that are in good physical condition, estrus usually occurs for the first time when they are only seven to eight months old. Males do not breed until their second autumn, when they are a year and a half old.

The does that survive winter in good condition will give birth to fawns from April to June, depending on the geographic location. A white-tailed fawn weighs five to six pounds at birth and, like the young of all hoofed animals, is born in an advanced stage of development. Within an hour of birth the fawn can walk and is led by its mother to protective cover before it can be discovered by a predator.

While does are tending fawns, adult bucks are growing new antlers. In September, after the antlers have reached their maximum growth for the year, they dry and harden. Then the cycle of life begins again with the rut.

# BEARS

# The Problem with Bears

BOTH BEARS AND PEOPLE are thriving in North America. That's the good news. In fact, both are doing so well that they are living in each other's habitats—people have moved into former bear country and bears have moved into cities and suburbs in pursuit of food. That's the bad news. Hungry bears are regularly entering backyards, patios, porches and decks, tearing down bird feeders, breaking into pet pens and opening garbage cans in search of food. They have even broken into houses.

Officials say that in 1998, nearly 2,400 bear sightings were reported in eastern Pennsylvania and northern New Jersey alone. In New Jersey, sightings had nearly doubled over the previous year, mainly because of an explosion in the bear population, which numbers about 10,000 animals in New Jersey and Pennsylvania combined.

Bear feeding has become a dangerous but popular pastime in Pennsylvania, inevitably leading to the detriment of both the people feeding the bears and the bears being fed. There are even reports of people inviting bears into their houses for a snack, in spite of officials' warnings that a 350-pound black bear is not a house pet.

# War Stories

※ In Vermont, a black bear crashed a neighborhood barbecue and refused to leave, according to a story in *USA Today*.

Bears that are fed in backyards become a greater threat, because they lose their fear of people and begin to expect food. When such bears are denied, they may become aggressive and dangerous.

❀ In Berlin, New Hampshire, wardens have counted up to 20 bears begging outside fast-food restaurants.

❀ New Jersey school children have been frightened by bears at bus stops.

❀ Pennsylvania homeowners have found bears hibernating under their patio decks and in backyard sheds.

❀ In Yosemite National Park, bears have broken into cars to get at picnic coolers.

❀ Michael Furtman was awakened one autumn night by something on the deck outside his home, which is located only five minutes from downtown Duluth, Minnesota. Getting out of bed quietly so as to not awaken his wife, Mary Jo, Furtman went to the window, drew back the drapes and was alarmed to find himself eye-to-eye with a huge black bear leaning on the window while ransacking a hanging bird feeder. "I could see the floor-to-ceiling window bowing inward under the weight of the leaning bear," Furtman recalled. "If the window had given way, the bear would have landed in my front room," he said.

He opened the door and sent his black Lab, Rascal, out to chase the bear. It worked. The bear ran off the deck and up a tree next to the house.

Furtman decided that the best thing to do was to remove the feeder. So in his bathrobe and slippers, he went out on the deck, took down the feeder and walked down the deck steps and out to the detached garage to store it.

Returning to the house, he found the bear back on the deck, between him and the only unlocked door to the house. He didn't have any keys, of course, in his bathrobe to let himself in at a different door. "I was stuck outside in the dark with a very annoyed and agitated bear," Furtman said. He decided that the best thing to do was to send Rascal after the bear a second time. The bear was now at the top of the stairs, however, and the only way for the courageous dog to chase it off the deck was to go up the same stairs that the bear would have to come down. "There was a lot of confusion for a few seconds, but the dog did get to the top of the stairs and the bear did come down and run off," Furtman said.

Hungry bears may enter backyards, patios, porches and decks, tearing down bird feeders, breaking into pet pens, and opening garbage cans in search of food.

Fortunately, Mary Jo slept through the whole incident and didn't hear about it until the next morning.

"We stopped feeding birds until we were sure that the bears were in hibernation," Furtman said.

✳ After a recent break-in by a bear looking for food, a woman in Jefferson Township, New Jersey, took action,

At campsites across the nation, black bears break into coolers, tents and cars in search of food. People should not feed bears, as they are large, unpredictable and powerful animals quite capable of harming humans.

according to Brian McCombie in *Field & Stream*. She installed metal bars over her ground-floor windows and rigged electric wire around the back porch. She stayed inside evenings and was even afraid to take out the trash, McCombie reported. Then came break-in number two. This time, the woman called the state Department of Natural Resources for help.

✱ Encounters with bears in Anchorage are common and increasing. Again, dog food, birdseed and garbage are just a few of the things that are drawing the bears into the city, according to a researcher who is studying black bears there.

The situation in Anchorage has become so troubling that 12 black bears in the past four years have been killed in the city in defense of life and property, according to the state Department of Fish and Game.

The department received some 1,800 complaints in 1998 from residents who reported bears in their yards, on porches, at bird feeders, in driveways, inside trash bins and on streets. A big problem is that bears get into garbage cans that are put out on the streets on trash days. The city is considering providing bear-proof trash containers as a possible solution.

🌠 "Finally, Dad found a feeder he was sure would lick the squirrel problem, Gwen Steet, Laurel Springs, New Jersey, told *Birds & Blooms* readers. "For several days, it did the trick and the birds dined in peace. Then late one afternoon, a loud noise disturbed my in-laws' dinner. They rushed to the back deck to discover a huge bear dragging the squirrel-proof feeder across the yard," she said. "Sure, Dad had beaten the squirrels, but now he had figure out how to beat the bears, too!"

🌠 In Rice Lake, Wisconsin, a black bear mauled a 14-year-old Boy Scout after dragging the tent in which he was sleeping from the campsite. The bear, later destroyed, was not afraid of humans. It had red ear tags that indicated it was a nuisance bear that had already been trapped and transferred out of the area.

# Solutions

First and most important, keep away from bears. Don't feed them. They are large, unpredictable, powerful animals that are capable of harming people. Bears that are fed in backyards become a greater threat, because they lose their fear of people and begin to expect food. When they are denied, they may become even more aggressive and dangerous.

Report any sighting of a bear in the backyard or neighborhood to a local wildlife agency. In most cases, a caller will be told to remove all food, including bird feeders, garbage and pet food to which bears may be attracted.

This first step is usually required before any further action, such as removing or destroying the offending animal, will be considered by the wildlife agency.

## BEAR CAUTIONS

The following is a list of precautions issued by the Wisconsin Department of Natural Resources concerning bears around homes:

- **Do not knowingly feed a bear.**
- **Reduce garbage odors by rinsing food cans before putting them in recycling containers or garbage cans.**
- **Compost vegetable scraps.**
- **Keep meat scraps in the freezer until garbage day and garbage cans in a closed building until pick-up.**
- **Remove bird feeders in the spring; if you do feed during the summer, remove suet and hummingbird feeders at night.**
- **Keep pet food inside.**
- **Keep barbecue grills and picnic tables clean.**
- **Use an electric fence to keep bears from beehives, sweet corn, fruit trees and berry patches.**

Noises may discourage bears. Either a loud radio or the kind of noisemakers or sound crackers that farmers use to keep deer and geese out of their crops may dissuade visiting bears. The noisemakers will, of course, frighten the birds, other wildlife and neighbors, too.

Keep in mind that bears hibernate in most of the country for at least five months during winter. Therefore, from about November to March, you can safely feed birds while the bears are sound asleep.

## IF YOU ENCOUNTER A BEAR

The Wisconsin Department of Natural Resources also advises the following if you happen to encounter a bear:

- **Don't panic, don't shoot the bear and don't approach it.**
- **Wave your arms and make some noise to scare the bear away.**
- **Back away slowly and go inside. Wait for the bear to leave.**
- **Spray the bear with a hose if you're at home.**

## BIRD FEEDER TRICKS TO DISCOURAGE BEARS

❀ When Linda D'Adamo of Forestburgh, New York, had a bear eating from her bird feeders, she asked for help from the readers of *Birds & Blooms* magazine. The suggestions she received included moving the feeders to a clothesline that is well out of reach of a bear, or hanging the feeders from a pulley system at least 10 feet off the ground.

# The Nature of the Beast

Black bears, the smallest of the three North American species—black, grizzly and polar—are the kind most likely to visit backyards. Standing, they average 40 inches at the shoulder and 60 to 70 inches in length. Males weigh 200 to 700 pounds; females are smaller. Though black is the most common pelt color, they also may be dark brown, cinnamon, blond, white and blue.

Bears are highly intelligent animals. Though they see well enough, they prefer to trust their more accurate sense

of smell. Their ability to smell food from a great distance is what leads them to backyard bird feeders, garbage cans and barbecue grills.

Except during mating and at locations of abundant food, like garbage dumps and salmon rivers, bears live solitary lives. Adult male back bears require large territories in which to find food and mates, ranging from 75 to 100 square miles; females range less.

A female with cubs is accorded a higher social status among bears than the same female without cubs. Fear of furious attack will cause even a dominant male to avoid conflict with a female that has cubs. The same respect should be granted by people.

Den sites of black bears include rock cavities, brush piles, hollow trees, root cavities, outbuildings and under patio decks. During winter sleep, denning bears are not in a typical state of hibernation. They are sensitive to their surroundings and can be easily aroused. While black bears may increase their daily intake from 7,000 to 20,000 calories to gain more than 100 pounds during the month before they den, they do not consume any food or water and do not urinate or defecate during their winter sleep. They lose 20 to 30 percent of their body weight while in winter sleep and their waste is converted back into useful protein. Unlike humans who might remain inactive for that length of time, bears do not suffer from osteoporosis.

Compared to other animals, bears have very low reproductive rates. Females require several years to become sexually mature and then they produce only two to three cubs once every two to three years. They breed in the spring or early summer, but the fertilized eggs undergo delayed implantation, so the birth occurs in midwinter while the mother is still in her den.

When born, black bear cubs weigh about 12 ounces. Until they are around 40 days old, bear cubs are deaf and blind. They remain with their mothers until they are nearly one and a half years old.

Old age for a black bear is ten to 12 years, though some have lived to be more than 20 and at least one survived to 30. Bears are aged by examining a cross section of tooth which contains microscopic growth rings, similar to those in a tree. Old bears often have problems with their teeth, which limits their food intake and results in ill health. Yet mortality in bears from human causes is usually much greater than from natural causes.

# RABBITS

# The Problem with Rabbits

ANY BACKYARD IN AMERICA with lush green grass, fragrant flowers, tasty vegetables and low-growing shrubs undoubtedly has rabbits—probably cottontail rabbits. Their appetite for fresh greens draws them to backyards, where they are bound to find not only an abundance of greenery, but birdseed as well.

Unfortunately, their consumption isn't limited to dainty nibbles of grass or tidying up spilled birdseed under feeders. Rabbits can do severe damage to young trees, especially fruit trees, in winter. In their desperation for food during this lean season, rabbits sometimes gnaw through the outer and inner bark of small trees, completely girdling the trunks and killing the trees.

The diet of a cottontail is almost infinite. "It will eat nearly every plant food that grows above the ground, a greater variety than that eaten by any other North American creature," according to the late John Madson in his Olin Mathieson Corporation book on the species.

# War Stories

✸ *Milwaukee Journal* reporter Harry Pease has first-hand knowledge of the propensity of rabbits to eat their way through a backyard. "Some years, the rabbits in my yard outnumber the flies and have appetites of dinosaurs," he said. "My neighbor watched a rabbit munch its way through an entire bed of forget-me-nots."

A cottontail's diet is almost infinite; it includes grass, flowers, vegetables, shrubs, and the outer and inner bark of small trees.

✻ "On a 25-acre tract in the East, cottontails once killed 12,000 young catalpa trees in a season. In an Iowa nursery, rabbits girdled and killed 3,000 fruit trees in a single tough winter," reported John Madson.

✻ When their outdoor motion-detecting spotlight went on, Jim and Martha Warren looked out the widow at the bird feeders in their Thomasville, Georgia, backyard to see what occurs nightly at many American feeding stations. There, sitting in the middle of a low tray bird feeder, was a fat cottontail, munching on the seed. That's what had been happening to the birdseed, Jim realized. "I'd been replenishing it every morning for the last week," he said.

# Solutions

## EXCLUSION

By far the best way to keep rabbits out of the garden is with low fencing. Chicken wire or hardware cloth two feet high and buried several inches should be effective. The same is true for protecting tree trunks and saplings from rabbits in winter. A ring of hardware cloth surrounding the vulnerable trunk, two to three feet high and several inches away from the bark, will exclude rabbits.

Bird feeders that are accessible to rabbits can be enclosed with large-mesh hardware cloth to cage out the offenders while still allowing the birds access to the food.

## REPELLENTS

Though there are many repellents that are said to be effective in protecting shrubbery from rabbits, most are limited by weather conditions and their adverse effects on the vegetation. Powdered aloe has been recommended as an effective rabbit repellent when dusted lightly from a shaker and reapplied after rains. Cayenne pepper applied liberally often works well, too.

## MYSTICAL BOTTLES

Under the category of "Old Wives' Tales" on how to keep rabbits out of the garden, here is just one example:

❁ "What are those jars doing in Katy's garden?" asked a friend who was visiting the elderly gardener's next-door neighbor. There were a dozen mason jars, each filled with red-colored water, placed at intervals along the border of the city garden.

With a straight face, Rick replied, "Katy says they keep the rabbits away." Seeing the look of incredulity on his friend's face, he added, "Think what you will, but Katy never has rabbits in her garden, yet the lady across the street has lots of them and they eat her vegetables."

As ridiculous as it may be, the mason jars filled with

red-colored water have also worked in gardens other than Katy's. Why they work is anybody's guess.

## TRAPPING AND TRANSPORTING

Rabbits are fairly easy to trap in live box-type or Havahart traps. Baited with the rabbit's favorite vegetable greenery, a well positioned trap will ensure a capture. Prisoners should be transported some miles away from the point of capture to guarantee that they do not return.

Rabbits are usually protected by law, so inquiries should be made with the state wildlife agency before undertaking any trap-and-transfer program for rabbits.

# The Nature of the Beast

Cottontail rabbits of one sort or another are found in every one of the lower 48 states, as far north as southern Canada and south into Central America. Cottontails prosper in a great variety of habitats, as long as there is an abundance of natural cover in which they can hide, nest and eat. They find security in hedgerows, thickets, weed clumps, shrubbery, stone walls and brush piles located in swamps, meadows, pastures, marshes, cemeteries, farmlands, old fields, open woodlands and backyards. They eat nearly anything green that grows.

The typical cottontail is covered with soft brown fur on its back and head and bright white fur on its breast and belly and on the underside of its short "cottontail." Its long ears are usually standing upright, its big eyes bulge and its velvet nose is constantly awiggle. It weighs between two and three pounds and stretches out to about 18 inches.

Cottontails are generally most active at dawn and dusk. They are usually solitary, except when breeding or when they are still young enough to be in nests.

A rabbit's hearing is acute. With the rabbit's ability to rotate its large ears, sounds can be picked up from front, back and side. It has excellent vision with oversized, protruding eyes. Its sense of smell, on the other hand, is not as well developed as in other mammals.

Perhaps the rabbit's best defense is its running game. "Running like a scared rabbit," is well put. With its incredible hind legs and back muscles, the cottontail can take 15 feet at a lick and dodge, twist and double back at top speed, mixing in 90-degree turns, like any great NFL running back.

In early spring, cottontails turn to another aspect of their survival—reproduction. In this behavior they are legendary. A female rabbit may produce three or four litters a year, with four to six young in each. In five years, a single pair of cottontails and their progeny (if they all survived), would number 350,000.

The behavior of breeding male rabbits is also legendary, as they compete—usually fight—for the right to breed the available females. They are often as "mad as a March hare!"

Just 30 days after breeding, the female rabbit gives birth in a ground nest that she has lined with grasses and soft fur plucked from her breast. Two weeks after birth, the little bunnies make their first forays out of the nest. At 16 to 20 days, the youngsters become independent and their mother is already preparing for another litter. Young females are ready to breed at just six months of age.

Though the shotgun is an effective deterrent to the rabbit, hunting has little effect on total rabbit populations. Predation (everything eats rabbits) and disease take a heavy toll. The mortality rate among young rabbits is as high as 80 percent, resulting in a life expectancy in the wild of less than one year.

# SKUNKS

# The Problem with Skunks

THE ONLY TIME MOST PEOPLE are aware of skunks is when they encounter the striped one's potent trademark perfume as it wafts on the wind for as far as a quarter of a mile. Because they are nocturnal, skunks are rarely seen and only occasionally smelled, which explains why there are more of them in backyards and gardens than might be realized.

Skunks can be unpleasant backyard guests for more reasons than their socially unacceptable odor. For one thing, they are grub eaters and it is not unusual for them to dig into the beautiful sod of a fine green lawn in search of food. Actually, skunks that create golfing divots in perfect lawns are doing the owner a favor by removing the harmful insect larvae, but that's a difficult point to make with an irate lawn groomer.

Dark, secluded dens appeal to skunks, so they may feel it's perfectly natural to crawl under a porch or deck for a daylight snooze or a long winter's sleep, in spite of the fact that the welcome mat is not out.

Skunks can also be carriers of rabies, particularly in the East and Midwest and along the Pacific Coast. As with raccoons, there are periodic outbreaks of the disease among skunks and they can pass it on to humans. A skunk seen during daylight may be sick and should be avoided even more than usual.

And, woe is the dog who happens to cross paths with a skunk.

A mother skunk carrying a baby in its mouth.

# War Stories

✳ "Berkeley was an English setter with a great nose," recalled Peter Harrison of Waukesha, Wisconsin. "In addition to pointing game birds, he often pointed turtles, rabbits, chipmunks and even butterflies."

One dark evening while being taken on his nightly walk, Berkeley discovered a new attraction. Unfortunately, Peter didn't know what Berkeley was pointing until it was too late. Berkeley had discovered a skunk in a grassy field and the two must have squared off, with poor Berkeley getting a full dose of skunk perfume right in his face.

"As the dog came out of the field, I knew immediately what had happened. He not only smelled to high heaven, but he was also partially blinded by the skunk's powerful spray," Peter related.

Peter tried one of the legendary antidotes for essence of skunk. He doused Berkeley with tomato juice, followed by a hosing down. It did little good. Peter then anointed the hapless dog with lemon aftershave lotion, but that didn't help much, either. So Berkeley spent the next couple of weeks in his outdoor kennel, airing out. For months afterward, every time that Berkeley got wet, he smelled of skunk.

✻ "After slaving over my lawn all last spring, fertilizing it, plucking dandelions and mowing it every few days, I awakened one morning to a war zone in my front yard," said Wally Wilkenson of Greensboro, North Carolina. "There were dozens of holes in my beautiful grass. It looked like someone was using my lawn for a driving range. If I ever get my hands on the culprit that did this, I'll strangle him," swore Wally.

The culprit was very likely a friendly neighborhood skunk out on the town in search of grubs, which were plentiful in Wally's perfect lawn. Fortunately for Wally, he would never get his hands on the culprit, for that would have been the mistake of his life.

✻ "I don't know what to do about the terrible smell from under the porch," lamented Anne Jackson of Monroeville, Pennsylvania. "I know it's a skunk, but I never see it. Sometimes it's worse, sometimes it's not so bad, but I can smell it almost all the time," she complained.

# Solutions

Whatever you do, do it with extreme care.

## LOCK IT OUT OF ITS HOUSE

If you have a skunk denning or snoozing under your porch, outbuilding, garage or anywhere nearby, the simplest solution is to close off its entrance while the skunk is

Because they are nocturnal, skunks are rarely seen and only occasionally smelled. A skunk seen during daylight may be infected with rabies and should be avoided!

out. Chicken wire makes a good exclosure for skunks. By sealing off the skunk's den site, the interloper will be forced to relocate.

## TRAP WITH CARE

The digging problem is more difficult to solve. Some people recommend the use of pesticides to rid the lawn of grubs, but that is a harsh and dangerous solution that threatens the lives of other wildlife. Trapping with a Havahart-type live trap and transporting the skunk may be a better solution. The trapping part is easy. Transporting it away from the property is much more tricky. The trapping and transfer of skunks is best left to animal-removal or pest-control experts, which are listed in the Yellow Pages.

A sure-fire bait for the trap is sardines or other canned fish. Expect the culprit to be caught at night, as skunks are nocturnal. Expect, also, to trap a variety of other critters that will be interested in the fishy bait, including opossums, raccoons, rats and the neighbor's free-roaming cat.

Don't attempt to trap a skunk unless you are experienced in the use of live traps and know how to take precautions to avoid being sprayed or bitten. If you find a skunk in the trap, a cautious, slow, quiet approach is highly recommended. Wear throw-away clothing, just in case. Slowly place a cloth cover over the trap and then lift it slowly and quietly into the transport (preferably not an enclosed one). Soft murmurs to the skunk may help, too. Release the skunk on Uncle Charlie's farm, in the same quiet, gentle manner. To accomplish all of this without getting sprayed will require extreme prudence and an enormous amount of luck. Remember, you can hire a professional to take the risk for you.

In some states, skunks are protected. Check with your state wildlife agency before starting to trap and transfer skunks.

## THE CHALLENGE OF SKUNK ODOR

❀ Dogs, cats and people sprayed with skunk scent are impossible to clean up totally. Contrary to popular belief, tomato juice, vinegar, bleach or ammonia are not the most effective remedies for a direct hit from skunk spray. Alkaline laundry soap, like Fels Naptha, works better, according to Dr. William Wood, a chemistry professor at California's Humboldt State University. But so far there is nothing that will do the job quickly and thoroughly. Skunk musk contains oily sulfur and thioacetate molecules. When the musk is sprayed, the thioacetates react slowly with water from the air or from the body of the victim, turning into a thiol that generates long-term odor.

A commercial deodorizer, Neutroleum Alpha (NA), available from U.S. Fish and Wildlife Service offices, claims to effectively mask skunk odor. Diluted in water, it may be used on pets or people, or to deodorize walls,

Contrary to popular belief, tomato juice, vinegar, bleach or ammonia are not the most effective remedies for a direct hit from skunk spray. Alkaline laundry soap, like Fels Naptha, or a commercial deodorizer will work better, but it may take months for the smell to leave completely.

floors, furniture or buildings that have been sprayed. Other commercial products available in some areas include Odor-Sol and Skunkoff.

## The Nature of the Beast

All four skunk species—striped, spotted, hognose and hooded—are native to North America and they all have scent glands. The striped is the most widespread, ranging from Canada, throughout the U.S. and south to Honduras. A cat-sized animal, the striped skunk's long black fur is marked with white, starting in a thin line between the eyes, broadening to a wedge at the back of the head, then separating into two lines running down the back and usually onto the tail.

Some have less white than others. A skunk's legs are rather short, its snout is pointed and the ears are small.

Skunks live in open woodlands, brushy fields and urban, suburban and rural backyards. They are omnivores, eating virtually everything from fruits and vegetables to insects, small mammals, birds and the eggs of birds and turtles. Because they are nocturnal, they are usually smelled rather than seen.

Obviously, the most unique feature of the striped skunk and its kin is that powerful weapon that puts down all challengers—a twin-nozzled scent gland that carries the strongest-smelling potion in the animal world.

This highly effective defense mechanism somewhat compensates for the skunk's inability to swiftly flee from danger. Its slow, ambling gait covers about one mph. In a hurry, it can achieve a top speed of about six mph.

In the North during the coldest period of the winter, skunks sleep alone or in family groups in dens such as an abandoned woodchuck, fox or badger hole, or in a rock pile, wood pile, hollow stump or log or under a building. It's when they select a building under which to hide or den that they get into the most trouble with humans.

Four to six young are born in April or May, after a 63-day gestation. At six weeks of age, the young venture from the burrow and are foraging for themselves by mid-summer. They remain with their mother through the first winter. In the spring, the yearlings leave to seek new territories, sometimes in suburban backyards.

The average life span of a skunk is only one or two years in the wild. In captivity, they have lived up to ten years.

# CHIPMUNKS

# The Problem with Chipmunks

THE CHIPMUNK IS THE JEKYLL and Hyde of the American backyard. While it is a devilish charmer and frisky dynamo that provides seemingly endless amusement for some people, others see it as a hoarder, hog and bully that brings only aggravation. The chipmunk can charm the dickens out of you and decimate your garden at the same time.

It is energetic and lightening fast, with a phenomenal work ethic. It will toil from morning to night, making countless trips between a bird feeder and its den, cheek pouches bulging with the best birdseed money can buy. The seed is not eaten by the chippy, at least not at the moment. It is being stashed for winter rations. Pound after pound of birdseed can disappear down a single chipmunk's burrow. If there are several chipmunks in the backyard, it can become rather costly to support the little thieves.

Gardeners tear their hair out trying to keep chipmunks from nibbling on ripening fruit. Strawberries seem to be a particular favorite.

# War Stories

❀ "Those blasted chipmunks eat more seed than the birds," ranted Martin Beckworth of Amherst, Massachusetts. "I'm convinced that if I dumped a truckload of bird-

Authors Note: Though this chapter is devoted entirely to the eastern chipmunk, it can be applied to all ground squirrel species of North America.

Cute, frisky, and industrious, a chipmunk can charm the dickens out of you and decimate your garden at the same time.

seed on my patio in spring, the chipmunks would have it all down their holes by fall."

✳ "Every spring, we plant our patio borders with colorful geraniums, impatiens and marigolds," said Patty Jones of Bethesda, Maryland. "As fast as we plant them, the chipmunks excavate them, successfully captivating us all the while," she said.

✳ "We gave up vegetable gardening because of chipmunks," explained Robert Cullen of Rosemont, Connecticut. "We tried to protect the strawberry patch by laying a single layer of cheesecloth over it and it did keep the birds out but not the chipmunks. Those rascals didn't even wait for the strawberries to ripen. As soon as the berries began to show a little red, the chippies slipped under the cheesecloth and attacked without mercy. After several more years of frustration, we finally plowed the patch under," he said.

✳ A farmer in Michigan was hoodwinked by a chipmunk, according to *National Wildlife* magazine. Described as a man who had no sympathy for rats, mice, crows and squirrels when it came to protecting his granary, he would shoot any of them on sight. However, one day he became so enamored of a chipmunk stuffing its cheeks with grain in his wheat bin that he found himself counting the intake rather than shooting the culprit. He got to 145 kernels before he realized he was being burglarized while he watched. Still he could not shoot. Later he told a friend, "I just stood there and enjoyed being taken."

# Solutions

Controlling chipmunks is not easy, partly because there are so many of them and partly because they are clever in their thievery.

### TRAPPING

Chipmunks, like squirrels, are backyard opportunists, but may be even more difficult to deter.

❀ "I finally had it," said Marshall Hencken of Pittsburgh, Pennsylvania. "The chipmunks were into everything and I decided to do something about it." So, Marshall began trapping chipmunks in small Havahart traps baited with peanut butter. After a summer of trapping and transporting 46 chipmunks many miles away and across a major interstate highway, Marshall realized to his great dismay that he had just as many chipmunks around his patio and garden as he had before he began his trapping scheme. "I believe that each time I removed one animal from the backyard, another one moved in," he explained. It was an apparent case of the natural vacuum at work, in which

Putting out food just for chipmunks, as for squirrels, may be the best way to keep them from hoarding your birdseed.

there was always another chipmunk on the outskirts ready to move into the prime habitat of Marshall's backyard.

Killing traps should be avoided because of the danger to other wildlife, such as robins, which are just as likely to take the bait as a chipmunk. The same is true of placing poisons around an area, as any animal might be tempted to take the bait.

Chipmunks are protected by law in some states and inquiries should be made with the state wildlife agency before trapping and transporting chipmunks.

## BAFFLE THEM

Chipmunks are much like squirrels in their eating habits but are not the jumpers that squirrels are. This makes it relatively easy to keep chipmunks off bird feeders by placing baffles above or below the feeders.

Likewise, chipmunks are heavier than most songbirds and their weight will lower the feeding treadles on weight-loaded feeders, effectively cutting off their access to the bird food.

## FENCING IS FUTILE

Chipmunks are small enough and cunning enough to beat almost any fence, either by passing through it, climbing over it or digging under it.

## REPELLENTS

Some people have had success keeping chipmunks off flowers and backyard vegetable gardens with a liberal dousing of cayenne pepper on the plants, but the hot substance must be replenished each time it rains. There are also commercial sprays that can be used, but caution must be exercised when using these chemicals on edible crops.

# The Nature of the Beast

The eastern chipmunk is a small, attractive, ground-dwelling, solitary diurnal rodent that weighs about three ounces. The flattened, well-haired tail is about a third of its total length of nine to ten inches of fur-covered energy. A chipmunk's orange-brown to chestnut body is marked with five stripes down the back. A creamy buff strip separates the dark stripes on the sides.

A chipmunk in a hurry holds its tail vertically as it scoots through flower beds, over rock walls and into woodpiles. Its head is rather short and its ears are rounded and flattened. Like other rodents, it does most of its damage with two gnawing teeth above and two below. The chipmunk's four clawed toes and thumbs equip it for holding food while sitting in an upright position. It has fur-covered cheek pouches into which it can put unbelievable amounts of food and other material.

In addition to their love of birdseed, bulbs and garden produce, chipmunks eat acorns, hickory nuts, beechnuts, cherry pits and various kinds of wild berries and weed seeds. Chipmunks also raid birds' nests, eating eggs and small young.

Of course, chipmunks chip, but they also make other sounds, including trills, whistles, chatters and warbles.

Chipmunks will eat birdseed, bulbs, garden produce, acorns, hickory nuts, beechnuts, cherry pits and various kinds of wild berries and weed seeds. Chipmunks also raid birds' nests, eating eggs and small young.

Communication is important to chipmunks. Even though they are solitary most of the year, they live in burrows close to other chipmunks and verbal exchanges are common.

Perhaps the best suited of all wild animals for life in a suburban backyard, the chipmunk is at home in fence rows, rock walls, wood piles, gardens and shrub thickets. The average home range of a single chipmunk is about one acre. Home ranges overlap and change in size and shape as the seasons and availability of food change.

Chipmunks are active from dawn to dusk in most warm weather. They can easily climb trees, especially if there is a bird feeder or bird nest to be raided.

When not above ground gathering and hoarding food, they are in their extensive burrows, which consist of about 12 feet of tunnel leading to several rooms used for sleeping, storage and latrine.

Unlike tree squirrels, chipmunks are inactive during winter months, disappearing in October or November and reappearing in March or April. Their winter quarters are their summer quarters sealed up. Inside, they sleep for a week or so at a time but are not true hibernators. They awaken to eat from their extensive larders and then resume sleep for another week or so. On particularly warm days in winter, chipmunks may emerge for a brief spell and then return to their chamber for more sleep. Some never awaken in the spring. Whether they have frozen, starved or just stopped breathing, it seems that death during winter sleep is a part of the chipmunk way of life.

Those that do awaken from winter sleep do so with breeding on their minds. Males are up and about a couple of weeks before females. When females arise, they are in heat almost immediately. Males approach the burrows of females with great caution, because females are very fussy about their mates and many a brash male has been beaten up. Sometimes when several males pursue a female at the same time, a chase will follow, with the female leading the pack. Courtship is brief: mating occurs in one or two minutes. The pair may remain together for another hour or so before the female drives her mate away.

After a 31-day gestation period, three to five babies are born in a leaf nest inside the mother's burrow. Each weighs about a tenth of an ounce, is blind, naked and completely helpless. They are weaned at about four weeks and leave the burrow in about six weeks. Some weeks later, each youngster is turned away from the natal den to pursue its own life in a new home range where it will dig its own burrow. During this period of change, the established chipmunks can be heard chipping a warning to all wandering newcomers. The message being transmitted is that the territory they've entered is already claimed, so move on!

Most chipmunks live only a little over one year, though in captivity they have lived to be eight to 12 years old.

One reason for the short life span in the wild is that chipmunk is high on the menu of many predators, including hawks, raccoons, foxes, coyotes, weasels, snakes, cats and dogs.

# HAWKS

# The Problem with Hawks

THE RAIDING OF BIRD FEEDERS by hawks has become a common and everyday occurrence in many backyards as the populations of birds of prey prosper. During one winter, the Cornell Laboratory of Ornithology related that 45 percent of predator "instances" reported at North American bird feeders involved hawks. In 1993, 19.5 percent of the participants in Cornell's Project FeederWatch reported sharp-shinned hawks at their bird feeders while 10.7 percent had Cooper's hawks, a significant increase over the figures tabulated five years earlier.

Migration counts at Hawk Mountain Sanctuary in eastern Pennsylvania and at Cape May, New Jersey, support this. "Cooper's hawks have shown a steady increase in numbers migrating past Hawk Mountain in eastern Pennsylvania since the late 1970s," reported biologist Laurie Goodrich. "And, except for a dip in the late 1980s and early 1990s, sharp-shinned hawk numbers have increased steadily as well," she said. This is despite the fact that a significant number of both species are not migrating south in the fall. According to annual Christmas bird counts administered by the National Audubon Society, growing numbers of sharp-shinned and Cooper's hawks are overwintering in northern regions from which they had traditionally migrated in the past. Many of those are hanging around near bird feeders, where a dependable supply of prey is available to them.

"Cooper's hawks are certainly thriving in Wisconsin," stated Dr. Robert Rosenfield, associate professor of

Sometimes one backyard pest controls another, as with this red-tailed hawk that has preyed upon a gray squirrel.

biology at the University of Wisconsin, Stevens Point, who has monitored the bird for the last 18 years. "They're bathing in people's birdbaths and nesting in their backyards, many 20 to 45 feet high in pines," he said.

It should be no surprise that studies of the raptors' eating habits show why backyard bird feeders have become fast food outlets for some hawks. "Our food studies of sharp-shinned hawks during the breeding season in Wisconsin showed that 95 percent of their prey items were small birds, primarily white-breasted nuthatches, black-capped chickadees and downy woodpeckers," reported biologist Eugene Jacobs, who has studied the breeding behavior of sharp-shinned hawks in Wisconsin for eight years.

## War Stories

❋ In the stillness of the frosty Ohio winter afternoon, Henry and Sue Strunk saw and heard what resembled a small explosion at their feeding station. Every bird on or near the feeders had erupted into the air, several striking the windows in their panicked flight. One, a dark-eyed junco, lay stunned on the snow, about to become the victim of the sharp-shinned hawk that had swooped onto the patio, causing the feeding birds to flee in terror. The hawk had skillfully staged another ambush. The stunned junco was easy prey.

✳ Panic-stricken songbirds thudded against my picture windows, desperately trying to escape an attacking Cooper's hawk, but one of the mourning doves wasn't fast enough. It was now grasped firmly in the hawk's talons, destined to become another meal that the majestic raptor had snatched from my feeding station.

# Solutions

All birds of prey, including the hawks that raid bird feeders in the backyard, are protected by federal and state laws and may not be harmed or killed, nor may their nests and young be disturbed.

## PLANT COVER

The only acceptable way to protect feeder birds from hawks is to plant abundant food and cover vegetation to provide concealed nesting sites for the songbirds as well as

Providing plenty of cover near bird feeders is the best way to prevent songbirds from predation.

escape routes and hiding places for birds when they are attacked.

Place bird feeders and bird baths in or near the natural cover, but do not hide them so much that they cannot be seen from inside the house.

Often, the best solution when hawks hang around your backyard is to simply live with them. As predators, they are a part of a balanced ecosystem and are simply doing what comes naturally.

✿ "I get a lot of calls from backyard bird watchers asking what can be done about the hawks that are attacking birds in their backyards," biologist Eugene Jacobs reported. "I tell them that by providing ample cover near the feeders, they will be giving the birds a better chance of surviving hawk attacks," said Jacobs. "Otherwise, I tell them they should enjoy watching these magnificent hawks at close range."

## DESPERATE MEASURES

If all else fails, a more drastic solution is to remove all bird feeders for a week or two. Hopefully, the hawk will move on and the feeders can be replaced.

## LIVE WITH THEM

In a sense, the bird feeders are there to feed birds and the hawks are birds that are attracted to the bird feeders for an easy meal. As predators, they are a part of a balanced ecosystem and are simply doing what comes naturally. The best solution is to live with them and appreciate their skills and their role in nature. Much of the time, a hawk will eventually leave the vicinity.

# The Nature of the Beast

Hawks are birds of prey that capture their victims with their strong feet, which are equipped with sharp, curved talons. Once they have seized their prey, most hawks will pluck it or tear it apart with a strong, hooked beak which features a curved and sharply tipped upper mandible. Owls and a few hawks may swallow small prey whole without bothering to pluck it. Later they cough up pellets containing the indigestible matter such as fur, feathers and bones.

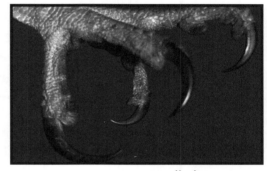

Hawks possess sharp, curved talons that pierce their victims' vital organs on impact.

Though a hawk is distinguished by the long, strong wings that make it an efficient and powerful flying machine, its visual ability is legendary, giving rise to the term "hawk-eyed." Its eyes are larger in proportion to its head than those of other animals, including man. A hawk directs its vision by moving its head, which can rotate nearly 360 degrees and employs both binocular and monocular vision. Binocular vision is important for hunting, providing estimated positions of the hawk's ever-moving prey.

Apparently, it also has something of a telescopic ability that gives it a long "focal length" like that of a telephoto camera lens. There is evidence that hawks can see objects that are three times farther away than can be seen by humans.

Their hearing is also acute, but we do not know as

much about the hearing ability of hawks as we do about the hearing ability of owls.

Hawks employ various hunting strategies. Accipiters—northern goshawk, sharp-shinned and Cooper's—are the hawks that most often hunt in backyards. Their shorter, rounded wings are useful for rapid wingbeats as well as for gliding. Typically, they hunt by waiting in a tree or other observation site, quietly watching for the right moment to attack.

When prey is sighted, the agile bird is able to attain top speed in merely a few quick thrusts of its wings, then it collapses its wings and streaks in silence to the kill. On impact, the victim is seized by sharp talons that instantly pierce vital organs. Northern goshawks customarily take their prey to what is known as a "butcher's block" to pluck and skin their food.

The sharp-shinned hawk is bluish-gray above and barred brown and white below. The smaller size and the squared (not rounded) tail of the sharpshin are the most reliable field marks to distinguish it from the Cooper's hawk. In its habitat of large and remote woods from southern Canada through the United States, the sharp-shinned hawk captures small to medium-sized birds, mice and shrews.

Like the sharp-shinned hawk, the larger Cooper's hawk is bluish gray above and barred brown and white below. The best field mark for distinguishing it from the sharp-shinned, apart from its greater size, is its rounded tail. It favors deciduous and coniferous woodlands over much of the United States and southern Canada, where it preys on birds and small mammals and has an undeserved reputation as having a taste for chickens. A female Cooper's is one-third larger than a male and its size and aggressive behavior intimidate its mate. So much so, that the male does nearly all the hunting for the pair. Even when they begin the 30-day incubation of their four or five eggs and the male continues to procure most of the food for the family, he rarely, if ever, carries it directly to the nest. Instead, he announces his arrival at a plucking post near the nest and then gets out of his mate's way as she retrieves the food.

The northern goshawk, North America's largest accipiter, is pale gray below and blue-gray above, with a black crown, a white streak over its eye and a rounded tail. In its forest habitat in Alaska, Canada and the northern United States, the goshawk preys on grouse, pheasants, ducks and snowshoe hares. In suburban backyards, mourning doves and pigeons are its primary prey.

The fastest of all hawks, falcons include the small, beautifully marked American kestrel that also frequents backyards and is only slightly larger than a robin. Falconlike in shape—short neck, small bulletlike head and slender, pointed wings—both sexes have reddish backs and tails and dark vertical whisker-like marks on the sides of the heads. Previously, it was known as the "sparrow hawk," because of its ability to capture house sparrows around farms. Sparrows now make up a relatively small part of its diet. One analysis of 685 kestrel pellets showed that mammals occurred in 66.8 percent of them (mostly meadow voles); insects (grasshoppers and beetles) in 66.1 percent; birds in 22.5 percent, mainly starlings and sparrows; and green snakes in 6.3 percent.

American kestrels are common backyard predators.

# RATS

# The Problem with Rats

RAT IS A DIRTY WORD to most people, reinforced by such expressions as, "you dirty rat," "I smell a rat," "a rat's nest" and "the rat race," suggesting a less-than-endearing attitude toward any mammal known as a rat.

This ugly reputation is due entirely to the behavior of two foreign species—the black rat and the Norway or brown rat—that invaded our shores hundreds of years ago, bringing destruction and carrying diseases such as typhus and plague. The Norway is the more abundant of the two alien rat species in North America and the more destructive.

Norway rats have been known to bite babies in their cribs and even attack sleeping adults. Elephants in zoos have had their toes chewed off.

Being bitten by a rat is a particularly nasty and potentially life-threatening experience, because they may be carrying one of several diseases that can be transferred to humans with catastrophic results. Two-thirds of the rats captured in Baltimore, for example, were found to have been infected with a hantavirus, according to Dr. James E. Childs of Johns Hopkins Medical Center, who studied rats in the streets of Baltimore for several decades. Hantavirus causes hemorrhagic fever and is a serious and often fatal disease in many Asian countries. The disease was contracted by humans in New Mexico when they inhaled airborne particles of droppings from infected deer mice.

Among the many other transgressions of these unwelcome aliens is their habit of eating birdseed that falls from feeders. Because these unsavory characters are mostly

Baby rats are weaned before they are a month old and can themselves breed at two to four months, producing six to eight litters annually. Theoretically, one pair can produce 20 million descendants in just three years.

nocturnal by nature, they are not often seen by the unsuspecting people who feed birds in their backyards. The food just disappears. Yet, about every eight to ten years the rat population increases dramatically and then it is not unusual to see them out and about in broad daylight, vacuuming up the birdseed and suet on the ground under feeders. It is a sight that often revolts or frightens people to the point that they stop feeding birds.

This may be because those people know how tenacious and tough Norway rats can be, with almost supernatural abilities to survive. "They can plummet five stories to the ground and scurry off unharmed; gnaw through lead pipes and cinder blocks with chisel teeth that exert an incredible 24,000 pounds per square inch; swim half a mile and tread water for three days; wiggle through a hole no larger than a quarter; and survive being flushed down a toilet and enter buildings by the same route," said *National Geographic* editor Thomas Canby.

# War Stories

❋ The first sight of a rat near a feeding station is always a shock. "There it was, right under the bird feeder, in broad daylight," said Joslin Hubert of Greensboro, North Carolina. "A huge brown rat with a long rat tail. I almost died at the sight of it," she said.

❋ "I heard that there was a rat invasion," said Olive Hazlett of Tarentum, Pennsylvania, "and because of the drought, they were coming up the sewer pipes. I'm keeping the lid on my toilet seat down," she said.

❋ Moscow authorities blame huge traffic jams caused by malfunctioning traffic lights on a plague of rats that are thriving beneath the Russian capital. The rodents had been eating through plastic-coated underground cables that control the signals, according to a report in the Rossyiskaya *Gazette*. The rats eat the cables more quickly then the understaffed traffic department can fix them, it said.

❋ The owner of a building destroyed by fire got little satisfaction from the fact that the rat responsible for short-circuiting the wires was probably killed in the blaze.

# Solutions

To totally rid an area of Norway rats, their shelter must be removed, all food supplies must be secured in rat-proof containers and the rats themselves must be destroyed.
If you have a bird feeding station, suspend the feeding operation until the rat situation is under control. The birds will quickly return when the feeders are back in place and

will find food in the wild and in other neighborhood bird feeders in the meantime.

## POISONS: EFFECTIVE BUT DANGEROUS

Possibly the most effective and most efficient way to control rats in the backyard is also the most dangerous—the use of poison. Rat poison, such as Warfarin or d-CON (effective even against rodents that are Warfarin-resistant), placed where the rats are eating birdseed, could be eaten by other animals, birds, pets, or even a child. If these poisons are used, they must be placed where only rats have access to them, which is extremely difficult to do.

## TRAPS ARE SAFER

A safer solution to a rat problem is the use of live traps, like Havahart, that allow you to see what has been caught before disposing of it. Bait the traps with the kind of food the rats are eating, such as sunflower seeds. Peanut butter spread on the release treadle is also inviting. Once the rat is trapped, keep the animal in the trap until it has been dispatched. This can be accomplished by putting the trap into water deep enough to drown the rat, by feeding the rat poison (dropped through the top of the trap), or by shooting it with a small caliber firearm such as a .22 rifle or a pellet gun, but not a BB gun because it is not powerful enough. Only after you are absolutely certain that the rat is dead should you open the trap. Wear gloves in all your dealings with rats. Even dead ones can spread disease.

Large snap traps also catch rats, but again, they may catch and kill other kinds of wildlife if they are set out in the open, including birds that feed from the ground. Like poison, killing traps should be placed only where no other wildlife will be killed by mistake.

## SHOOTING IS CHALLENGING

If you live in an area where shooting is permitted, this offers another option for disposing of rats. While a good shooter with an accurate firearm may make impressive dents in a rat population, removing them totally from an area using only a gun is challenging. Getting a bead on them is tough enough, but if they are shot at and missed, they are less likely to present themselves for a second shot. Pellet guns and .22 caliber rifles are most often the weapons of choice. BB guns are usually not powerful enough to kill rats. Obviously, shooters should be certain that the area behind a targeted rat is clear of people, pets, other wildlife and property.

## EXTERMINATORS TO THE RESCUE

If you fail to eliminate the rat problem or do not want to tackle it yourself, a professional exterminator can do it for you. Most exterminators are well trained and can get to the heart of the problem quickly, with limited danger to other wildlife. A qualified exterminator should rid the area of rats and/or other pest animals within a couple of weeks.

# The Nature of the Beast

Even in physical appearance, the brown (Norway) rat is unattractive. Its rather coarse hair may be black, brown or gray above and paler to gray or yellowish below. The large ears are hairless and the tail is long, scaly, ringed and nearly naked. It grows to 18 inches long and weighs up to two pounds. The evil nature of the beast is characterized by its slinking, furtive gait of only one to two miles per hour. It seldom attempts to climb and when it does, it climbs rather poorly. It can swim and dive well and can cross rivers of considerable width.

Somewhere within its 100- to 150-foot home range is its den. When not living inside a building, a rat will dig a shallow burrow about a yard in length and a foot deep. Baby rats are born in a crude nest after a gestation period of only 22 days. At birth, the six to 16 babies are undeveloped, hairless, blind, deaf and completely dependent on the care of their mother. Yet they are weaned before they are a month old and can themselves breed at two to four months, producing six to eight litters annually. Theoretically, one pair can produce 20 million descendants in just three years. They thrive everywhere man lives and will eat anything, even each other. This is why they have totally decimated native wildlife populations in many island ecosystems, including some in Hawaii and Galapagos.

Norway rats were probably first introduced into the U.S. as stowaways on ships from England well before the American Revolution. Since then, the species has been repeatedly imported into the country from all parts of the world until it is now found throughout the continent.

The species is more or less colonial and under favorable food and shelter conditions can reach dense populations. Rats are fast learners and will quickly adjust to nearly any effort to control their numbers.

Life expectancy of a young rat in the wild averages only three months, with less than 10 percent surviving a full year. Those that live to be a year old will go on to average two to three years longevity. Causes of death range from human rat control to rat fights and cannibalism to predation from larger mammals and birds of prey.

The only benefit realized by humans from these rattiest of rats is the breeding of albino Norways for scientific laboratories. White rats have actually become so manageable that the Kalamazoo (Michigan) College Rat Olympics are held annually in late August to challenge white rat athletes in several events, with a pound of cookies offered as a reward.

All rats are not dirty rats. There are at least 50 species of native North American rats that are handsome, clean and industrious animals, admired by biologists and others who know their true nature.

About the only trait our pleasant native rats have in common with the despicable aliens is two upper and two lower front gnawing teeth, which classifies them all as rodents.

# BULLY BIRDS

# The Problem with Bully Birds

IN THE MINDS OF MOST backyard birders, there are good birds and bad birds. The bad birds—jays, grackles, starlings, blackbirds, crows and pigeons—consistently monopolize bird feeders by chasing away the good birds and consume foods not meant for them.

Grackles, European starlings and red-winged black-birds can swarm into a backyard like an army of Darth Vaders in space crafts, blanketing the feeder trays and gobbling up the seeds in a noisy chorus of static.

A blue jay may swoop onto a feeder, sounding a blasting alarm that resembles a hawk's scream, sending goldfinches, juncos and chickadees fleeing in panic.

# War Stories

✻ A pair of crows watched from an oak tree as a robin carried a slender worm to its day-old chicks in a nest on the coach lamp at the front door of Mel and Linda Hanson's home on a lake just outside St. Paul, Minnesota. When the robin left the nest to get more food, the two crows dropped down and landed on the side of the nest. The Hansons watched in horror as the crows peered into the mud cup containing four blind and naked nestlings, picked up one at a time and swallowed them whole. When the nest was empty, they left. It happened so quickly and the Hansons were so dumfounded, they didn't have time to react.

In cities throughout the world, pigeons (or rock doves) have adapted well to the ledges of buildings, bridges and monuments, consuming bread crumbs and seeds offered by admirers.

The bird feeder in a Fort Lauderdale, Florida, backyard became a pigeon ghetto. It was so loaded with pigeons from morning to night, that it swayed back and forth as they clambered over one another to get to the birdseed mixture. The pigeons completely dominated the feeder and few, if any, other birds were permitted to feed. Eventually, the other birds seemed to stop passing through the yard to check on the availability of feeder food.

Even among a species as petite and desirable as hummingbirds, there are bullies, usually a territorial male that decides the sugar-water feeder is part of his domain and runs off all others of his species, with the possible exception of his own mates. Sylvia Bashline, of Spruce Creek, Pennsylvania, had a particularly aggressive rubythroat that she named "Guardbird," sometimes referring to him simply as "GB." He was the terror of the hummingbird feeder.

Birds can also be pests in gardens, as when blackbirds, crows, grackles and even the otherwise-welcome species such as robins and mockingbirds eat berries and vegetables just as they are ripening. "If they're going to eat my garden produce, I wish they'd eat a whole piece instead of just pecking off a few bits," lamented Kelly Gorman, Louisville, Kentucky.

These kinds of problems with pest birds have caused some people to simply throw in the towel after a while and stop feeding birds altogether. The solution need not be so drastic.

# Solutions

### EXCLUDE THEM FROM FEEDERS

✾ "Early one morning, I had starlings, grackles and red-winged blackbirds invade my neighborhood," said Sue Narkiewicz of Albany, New York. "They were all over my house and my neighbor's house, tapping on the gutters of the roof and on my bird feeders. When they swooped down across my yard, they scared all the smaller birds," she explained.

"I decided to do something about it, so I replaced one of my bird feeders with a Duncraft Haven, which is a tube feeder surrounded by a green cage. It allows little birds, like chickadees, tit-mice, nuthatches and finches to enter the cage

A bird feeder such as this tube feeder surrounded by a green cage, allows little birds in and keeps out the bully birds.

to reach the food, but the cage prevents larger grackles and redwings from feeding. Also, I changed from all-purpose seed in all the feeders to safflower seed only. These two steps seem to have solved the problem for me," Sue said.

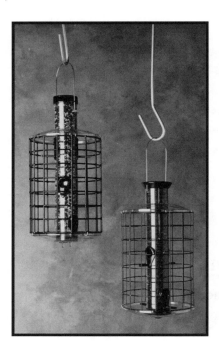

Although there are commercially made feeders that are already enclosed with mesh or a cage, you can enclose your own with large-mesh hardware cloth or chicken wire.

Because nearly all pest birds are larger than those that are considered to be more desirable birds, feeders can be adapted to accommodate only the smaller birds. By enclosing the feeders with large-mesh hardware cloth or chicken wire with openings large enough to allow the smaller birds to pass through, the larger birds will be excluded. As Sue Narkiewicz found out, there are commercially made feeders that are already enclosed with plastic-covered mesh to exclude pest birds—and squirrels—from seeds and suet.

## FOILING STARLINGS

❀ European starlings can be foiled at feeders in a couple of ways. Because of their fondness for suet, they can be discouraged if the suet feeder is hung up and under a domed squirrel baffle. Starlings are reluctant to venture underneath any kind of cover. A special starling-proof suet feeder, in which the suet can be eaten only from underneath, is a variation on this technique and many who feed backyard birds have found it to be quite effective.

## FOIL THE GROUND FEEDERS

❀ Marianne Colucci of Cedar Grove, New Jersey, had flocks of pest birds eating the seed that dropped from her hanging niger (thistle) seed feeder. "The pigeons and doves were eating the food on the ground and they were multiplying in numbers all over my yard," Marianne explained. "So I placed my garbage can directly under the hanging feeder to catch the seed. No pigeon or dove dared to fly into the garbage can and soon they were gone," Marianne said.

## HITCHCOCK'S BIRDS

❀ "I had problems with grackles, crows and blackbirds flocking to my feeders," said S. Lynn Cartee of Bessemer, Alabama. "My little birds didn't dare come when the crows were around. It sometimes looked like a scene out of the frightening thriller *The Birds*.

"To get rid of the pest birds, I changed to foods that

Starlings are reluctant to venture underneath any kind of cover, so a suet feeder that can only be accessed from below will keep them away.

Various types of scarecrows and loud noise-makers may keep problem birds and other critters out of your vegetable garden. What especially works are objects that move in the wind.

they don't like," Lynn said. "I quit putting out table scraps and I removed all the suet. For the finches, I now feed only the niger (thistle). And for cardinals, chickadees and nuthatches, I feed only safflower seed," she said. "The grackles, crows and blackbirds don't visit me anymore."

## SCARED OUT OF THE STRAWBERRY PATCH

❁ If birds are raiding your vegetable garden, scarecrows of various identities and loud noise makers may be successful in discouraging them. Grace Anderson Schrunk of Blain, Minnesota, told *Birds & Blooms* readers that she uses a clock radio tuned to a loud station to keep birds out of her strawberry patch.

❀ Most gardeners cover their plants with netting, but Emmylu Lawrence of Beaverton, Oregon, another *Birds & Blooms* reader, had a better idea. She bought some stuffed toys from the thrift store and hung them from stakes around the berries. She enjoyed the comedy of the birds sailing in for a bite of fruit and quickly flying away when they saw the toys moving in the breeze. Stuffed owls or hawks or even a toy snake should work just as well. In fact, any object that has eyes and moves in the wind should be an effective scarecrow.

## HUMMINGBIRD BULLIES

❀ Sylvia Bashline figured out how to thwart the male hummingbird that was chasing all the other hummers away. "What I finally did to give the other hummingbirds a chance to feed was to put up two more sugar-water feeders around the back of the house where 'Guardbird' couldn't see them," she explained. "He still guards his own feeder but he doesn't chase the others away from the feeders he can't see."

# The Nature of the Beasts

Most pest birds are gregarious; they socialize with other members of their kind and live most of their lives in flocks. For these birds, there is both safety and strength in numbers and when pest birds invade a backyard, they almost always arrive in a flock.

Only during the breeding season, from April to July, do these gregarious species live in pairs or small family groups, though most nest in loose colonies.

Jays, crows and magpies are all members of the crow family and as a group are among the most intelligent of birds. That, of course, makes them more difficult to deter from bird feeders and garden patches, because they are clever and often outwit the schemes meant to discourage them. They eat nuts, corn and suet at feeders, as well as fruits, vegetables insects, fish, salamanders and sometimes small birds and birds' eggs.

Red-winged blackbirds are also sociable birds that nest in loose colonies. The males set up territories on their breeding grounds in the spring before the females arrive and defend the new grounds vigorously against other males. When there is a surplus of females, males may be polygamous, sometimes having a dozen females to a harem. Three-quarters of a redwing's diet is cultivated grains, weed seeds, fruits and feeder bird foods; the balance is insects, spiders, mollusks and snails. In late summer, red-winged blackbirds form large flocks that remain together through fall, winter and spring migrations. It is during these flocking periods that they present the greatest nuisance in backyards.

Common grackles also spend much of the year in flocks. Even when nesting they live in colonies of 20 to 30 pairs. During fall, winter and spring migration, grackles gather with European starlings, red-winged blackbirds and brown-headed cowbirds, often in huge noisy flocks that roost together, sometimes disturbing people living nearby. The flocks can also cause damage to crops and wreak havoc at backyard bird feeders.

Originally native to Europe and Asia, the rock dove (city pigeon) is now found worldwide. It is a common pest at bird feeders where it may monopolize the food.

Another bird, enjoyed by many city park visitors but often considered a pest by those who feed backyard birds, is the 14-inch-long rock dove, also known as a barn or city pigeon. It is found in a variety of color forms that were developed through domestication. Yet most rock doves resemble their wild ancestors—gray overall with darker heads, iridescent purple necks and white rumps. The name "rock dove" comes from the attraction of the wild birds to rocks, cliffs and ledges in their native Europe and Asia. In cities throughout the world, they have adapted well to the ledges of buildings, bridges and monuments and to the lofts and beams of barns in the countryside, often making themselves pests. Rock doves eat grains and green sprouts on farms and consume bread crumbs and seeds in cities and at backyard bird feeders. They are a common pest at bird feeders when they monopolize the food and discourage other birds from feeding.

# WOODCHUCKS

# The Problem with Woodchucks

WOODCHUCKS ARE ALWAYS a surprise visitor to the back-yard. These balls of fur with flat heads are typically residents of farm fields. But as shrinking farmland is replaced by homes with backyard wildlife habitats, many wood-chucks are lured into suburbia where they find plenty of room for digging and a bounty of tasty offerings in vegetable and flower gardens.

# War Stories

❋ Sue Adams called, "Come with me—and hurry!" to her neighbor who was the local wildlife authority in their northern Illinois community. "Sparky's chasing an animal. We think it's a beaver!"

The nature expert arrived just as a dark brown animal ran up a small tree, with Sparky close behind. By this time, quite a crowd had gathered because word had spread that there was a beaver in Sue's front yard. As soon as the wildlife expert saw the animal, her hunch was confirmed. It had no beaver tail. However, the buck teeth and sable coat were undoubtedly what convinced the assemblage that this was a beaver.

As Sue tried unsuccessfully to get her excited German shepherd away from the base of the tree, the furry animal panicked and scrambled back down the tree headfirst. It covered less than four feet before the dog had it by the scruff of the neck.

Many woodchucks are lured into suburbia where they find plenty of room for digging and a bounty of tasty offerings in vegetable and flower gardens.

When Sparky finally released the lifeless creature, the nature expert showed the neighbors the identifying characteristics of a woodchuck.

"Do you think this is the animal that has been eating my garden vegetables lately?" Sue asked.

"Quite possible," said the nature expert.

"Well, good for you, Sparky," Sue announced. "But I would never have guessed that a beaver would eat garden vegetables," she added as she disappeared into her house.

❋ Marilyn Jacobs said to her husband, "Take a look at this. Something has been eating the impatiens." Sure enough, some animal had made a meal of the lush flowers that were in full bloom at their Springfield, Missouri, home.

The Jacobs decided to keep an eye on the impatiens and later that day they spotted the perpetrator. At first, the brown furry animal was a mystery to them, but a book on animals told them that the creature was a woodchuck, also called a groundhog.

In Jamestown, New York, Gloria Johnson's strawberries were almost ready for picking when she found her garden a shambles. "It looked like a drunken bulldozer drove through it," she said. Right in the middle of the devastation was a mound of fresh soil and the hole from which it had been dug.

Her local agricultural extension agent told her that she had a woodchuck in residence and as long as there were strawberries to eat, the chuck would be staying on.

In Sequoia National Park a few years ago, woodchucks developed exotic tastes. They were eating the radiator hoses and electrical wiring on cars parked by visitors hiking the High Sierra.

"They have no trouble entering the engine compartment from under the car," a park official told the *Wall Street Journal*. "Then, they chew on things."

When the owner of an Alfa Romeo turned the key in the ignition, the electrical system promptly shorted and burned the protective covering on the wires that had been eaten away. He had to have the vehicle towed to Bakersfield, 150 miles away, for repairs.

Another motorist driving away from the park noticed that his engine was overheating. He stopped, lifted the hood and found a woodchuck huddled on the engine block and a radiator hose that had been chewed through.

After a dozen automobiles had been hobbled by woodchucks, rangers began trapping them in the parking lot and transporting them to remote areas of the park. The bait for the traps? Old car radiator hoses!

The common woodchuck, alias groundhog, will eat up to 1.5 pounds of greens every day. They are particularly fond of garden beans, peas, herbs, tomatoes, strawberries and flowers such as impatiens, pansies and petunias.

# Solutions

If you have woodchucks in your garden, there are several ways you can attempt to control them, including fencing, repellents and trapping.

## FENCE THEM OUT

Fence the vegetable garden with chicken wire or hardware cloth that is at least three feet high and buried about a foot to prevent the woodchucks from digging under it. Stake the fence every few feet to add strength. If you bend the top of the fence outward, it should keep the woodchucks from climbing over.

## REPEL THEM

Another deterrent is the use of cayenne pepper on flowers and vegetables. By sprinkling the hot red pepper liberally on the plants that the woodchuck is eating, you should deter further munching. It has worked well on impatiens, petunias and other flowering plants.

## CHASE THEM

Certain breeds of dog, such as German shepherds and terriers, are natural pursuers of animals like woodchucks. They rarely need coaxing to chase a woodchuck each time it appears. If the dog catches the animal, it will usually kill it quickly.

## TRAP AND RELOCATE THEM

And finally, trapping the offenders is a possible solution. With a Havahart live trap, woodchucks are fairly easy to trap, especially if they are youngsters. For bait, use the same plants to which the woodchucks have been attracted. Apples, carrots, lettuce and sunflower seeds are other possible baits. Be sure to release the offender several miles from the scene of the crime, or it may find its way back.

❀ Trapping was how Frank and Pat Dentice of Wauwatosa, Wisconsin, tackled the situation when they spotted a woodchuck sitting up in their backyard vegetable garden. "He was eating the tomatoes from the bottom up and various flowers were being stripped," Frank said.

He baited a Havahart trap with sunflower seeds that he poured in a 10-foot line from where the 'chuck had been eating tomatoes to the treadle of the trap. "I sat in my living room and watched as the woodchuck ate his way up to and into the trap. I heard the door fall and I had him," Frank said.

The woodchuck was transported some distance away to a city park, where it presumably found plenty of green grass on which to munch. There have been no further sightings of woodchucks in the Dentice garden.

Be sure to check with your local wildlife agency for any restrictions concerning the trapping and transportation of woodchucks.

# The Nature of the Beast

The common woodchuck, alias the groundhog, is a rodent, or gnawing mammal, belonging to the marmot family, which includes its high country western cousins, the yellow-bellied and hoary marmots. Marmots belong to the larger family of squirrels, composed of prairie dogs, ground squirrels, chipmunks and tree squirrels. They all have four toes on the front foot and five on the back.

The woodchuck has prominent large, chisel-like "buck" teeth that are sharp and strong.

The woodchuck's clawed feet are well suited for excavating engineer-quality burrows with at least two entrances, one of which is sometimes in the middle of a garden. A 'chuck may remove as much as 700 pounds of soil and rock to complete a 20- to 25-foot-long burrow with multiple chambers.

A fully grown woodchuck will be about two feet long from nose to tail tip and weigh five to 10 pounds, about the size of a large, well-fed house cat. It is covered with coarse brown fur. The closer it is to autumn, the fatter the woodchuck grows. By September, layers of fat hang so heavily on the woodchuck that its jelly belly drags on the ground.

As winter approaches, the woodchuck prepares for its long nap by sealing off the entrances to its burrow with several feet of soil. It then begins hibernation by undergoing a series of body changes to conserve fat. Its body temperature drops from 99° F to about 40° F; its heartbeat slows from 80 per minute to about five per minute; and its breathing is reduced from 12 to about four breaths per minute.

Few woodchucks emerge to bask in the glory that awaits them on February 2, Groundhog Day. Most remain snuggled in until March or April. A few are prodded out of their slumber long enough to satisfy a local newsman who feels obligated to give a meteorological forecast based on the folklore, "If the groundhog sees its shadow, there will be six more weeks of winter."

When woodchucks do emerge from their winter quarters in March or April, it is sex, not weather, that arouses them. Males travel the countryside in search of receptive females in their burrows. Scent tells them if the occupant is a female, male or a mated pair. When a suitable female is found, the suitor enters the burrow in the hope that the occupant will accept him and mate.

A pregnant woodchuck tolerates the presence of the father until shortly before the birth of her three to four young, about a month after breeding. At about six weeks of age, babies are weaned and start to explore the world outside the burrow. By the end of July, the youngsters are in search of a home territory of their own, which may be a backyard garden. They will remain solitary and are unlikely to wander more than a few hundred yards from their new burrows for the balance of the year.

Ever alert, woodchucks have keen eyesight and sensitive hearing. They are usually spotted sitting upright at the entrance to their burrows near a lush supply of green food, such as a vegetable garden. They will eat up to one and a half pounds of greens, including alfalfa, grass and clover, every day. They are particularly fond of garden beans, peas, herbs, tomatoes, strawberries and flowers, such as impatiens, pansies and petunias.

# OPOSSUMS

# The Problem with Opossums

THE DIM-WITTED OPOSSUM ranks low on the list of back-yard pests, simply because it causes few problems and can be controlled with very little effort.

Still, there are a few reasons why this primitive animal gets into trouble with gardeners, farmers and backyard bird watchers. For one thing, while opossums will eat almost anything, they are particularly fond of garden fruits and vegetables. They will never pass up birdseed either from an accessible tray feeder or from the ground where it has dropped beneath hanging and post feeders. In addition, anyone who still keeps chickens or ducks in hen houses has to guard against opossums.

# War Stories

✹ "I have a problem with opossums getting into the suet I prepare for the birds," Carolyn Williams, Murphy, North Carolina, reported in *Bird Watcher's Digest*. "They get it just after the sun goes down. So, I have to take the suet in each night then put it out again in the morning."

✹ "The automatic yard light came on and there it was, a big, fat opossum sitting in the middle of the bird feeder tray," said Tom Jackson of Deerfield, Michigan. "I wondered why the birdseed was disappearing from that feeder every night and now I know," he said.

Opossums will eat almost anything, including birdseed and garden produce.

❋ "I can't blame the 'possum," said Tim Fielding, Richmond, Virginia. "I didn't do a good job of fencing my garden. He got in through a big hole and then enjoyed himself eating his fill of squash. The problem was that when he was full, he couldn't find his way out of the fence and he was trapped. That's how I caught the thief red-handed," Tim said.

❋ "Sammy is a bird dog, but he's also interested in other smelly animals" reported Virginia Stiemke of Atlanta, Georgia. "When he cornered an opossum in our garden last winter, the poor animal rolled up and died of fright. We thought he really was dead," she said. "But an hour later, we saw the opossum come back to life and amble off into the woods."

## Solutions

If you have opossums in your garden or at your bird feeders, there are a number of strategies for attempting to control them.

## FENCING—MAYBE

Fencing the garden with chicken wire or hardware cloth may be effective, though opossums are better climbers than many garden pests. Bending the top of a three-foot-tall fence outward should help prevent the opossum from getting over it.

## HOT REPELLENTS

Cayenne pepper sprinkled generously on the plants that the opossum has been eating may discourage further damage, though opossums seem to eat anything and everything, hot or not.

## DEADLY CHASE

Some dogs, particularly those bred for hunting or for digging animals out of burrows, like terriers, are usually more than eager to chase small animals, but the opossum will probably react very differently from most animals. It is likely to "play dead." That will make it easier for the dog to catch, but a dog may react to a "dead" opossum by leaving it alone.

## EASY TO TRAP

Trapping is another option and is usually relatively easy. An opossum can be lured into a Havahart live trap with any kind of table scraps, fruits or vegetables. Take the opossum several miles away before releasing it to ensure that it does not return.

Check with your local wildlife agency for any restrictions concerning the trapping and transportation of opossums.

# The Nature of the Beast

The opossum is unique among the mammals of North America. For one thing, it is the continent's only marsupial. Like kangaroos, koalas, wombats and wallabies, the female opossum has a pouch in which she carries her young until they are weaned.

The average adult opossum is the size and weight of a house cat, about 24 to 26 inches long, including its 12-inch tail and weighs six to 12 pounds. It has jet-black eyes, a pink nose, naked black ears, a sharply pointed snout and a mouth that is full of teeth—50, which is more than any other mammal in North America.

Its long, grizzly gray coat can look well groomed or unkempt, depending on what the animal has been doing and where it has been. It has short legs for an animal of its size and each pale, pinkish foot has five toes, the first of which resembles a human thumb.

The opossum's eyesight is poor at best, but its sense of smell and touch are acute and its hearing is good, except in some low ranges.

It is a slow-moving creature that ambles at only eight mph at full speed. Perhaps to partly make up for this, it is at home in trees and maneuvers well among the branches with its grasping feet and prehensile tail.

Because it is nocturnal, the opossum is rarely seen abroad in daylight. When it is caught or cornered, an opossum may fall into a deathlike state as a defense mechanism. The expression "playing 'possum" comes from this unique ability to play dead.

Ideal habitat for opossums is woodland, farmland and suburban backyards near water. A hollow tree, log or abandoned burrow of a woodchuck, skunk or fox makes an acceptable den site for an opossum. The nest consists of

Solitary, except for females with young or for very brief interludes during the breeding season, opossums have little need to communicate and have very few vocalizations, except for an occasional hiss or click.

leaves carried into the den. The opossum diet includes almost anything organic, from garbage to birdseed to poisonous snakes, insects and ripening garden vegetables. Occasionally, opossums will eat wild bird eggs and nestlings.

Courtship among opossums is nearly nonexistent. The sexes merely encounter one another, mate and then continue on their way. The female gives birth to some 16 embryos, each less than ½ inch long. Each embryonic off-spring must then drag itself from the birth canal to the pouch, a distance of only three inches, but a long way for such an undeveloped newborn. Those that successfully make the trip, an average of nine, remain in the pouch for 75 to 85 days, where they nurse and grow continuously. After three months of living with their litter mates and their mother, young opossums strike out on their own, dispersing from the area.

# WOODPECKERS

# The Problem with Woodpeckers

WOODPECKERS, ALMOST ALWAYS, are delightful birds to have in backyards and at feeding stations. At times, however, woodpeckers cause problems when they drill holes in siding or roofs while looking for insects, creating storage holes for nuts or even trying to excavate a nesting cavity. In other cases, the birds may choose sites such as drain pipes, siding or chimney flashing for their drumming, making enough noise to shatter the serenity of the neighborhood.

There are three reasons why woodpeckers hammer on the sides of houses, buildings, utility poles and tree trunks. In the spring when other birds are singing to proclaim their breeding territories and attract mates, woodpeckers drum with their sturdy bills to broadcast their presence and to declare their control of the territory. If the drumming is on the side of a house, it may awaken occupants and cause damage to the building. Houses with metal siding often provide a better sounding board for woodpeckers than wooden siding.

At other times of the year, woodpeckers drill holes in the sides of houses to create nesting or roosting cavities in which they can raise young or keep warm. The damage to siding when woodpeckers create nesting and roosting sites is usually more extensive, because they chisel out deep, cone-shaped cavities.

The third reason for woodpeckers hammering on the sides of people's houses is to acquire or store food. If a woodpecker discovers that the siding on a house contains

Attractive and interesting to watch, woodpeckers cause problems when they hammer on siding, utility poles, and valued trees.

wood-boring insects, it is apt to drill the siding in many places to extract the insects from inside the wood. It can be rationalized that woodpeckers searching for food are actually beneficial to homeowners, removing the harmful insects that are causing damage to the house. They are also an early warning signal that tells the homeowner something needs to be done about the insects that are eating the wood. Some woodpeckers, especially acorn woodpeckers, are notorious for making a series of large holes in which to store their winter larder.

Researchers studying woodpecker damage in eastern Tennessee found that 94 percent of all woodpecker problems occurred from February to May (the courting and nesting season). The majority of the houses damaged were contemporary or ranch style and were located in subdivisions. Surfaces that were brown or natural in color were most frequently damaged. Unpainted surfaces received more damage than painted surfaces. Cedar was the wood most often attacked. In addition, the damaged houses commonly had woodlands of large hardwood trees located within a half mile.

# War Stories

✺ Many buildings suffer unwelcome attention from woodpeckers and Doris Mallory's reaction to the woodpecker tapping on her Columbia, Missouri, home, is typical. "Help! I have a woodpecker pecking holes in the side of my house," she complained. "How can I discourage this bird from pecking at my house and get it to move on? I don't want to hurt the bird, but the noise is annoying and the holes are getting bigger," she said.

✺ Early every spring morning, just as the sun was rising on their Sanibel, Florida, home, Sam and Emily Layton were rudely awakened by what sounded like a jackhammer reverberating through their house. It was a red-bellied woodpecker drumming away with gleeful abandon on the galvanized chimney flue. The woodpecker's hammering was particularly well amplified by the hollow metal and the bird seemed to thoroughly enjoy the racket it made.

Woodpeckers, like this red-bellied, hammer for three reasons: to proclaim their breeding territories and attract mates; to create nesting or roosting cavities; and to acquire or store food.

✺ An acorn woodpecker drilled a series of large holes in the side of Chet and Beverly Thiele's home in San Diego, California and then filled each with an acorn, giving a pockmarked look to that side of their house.

159

# Solutions

There are many creative ways to deal with the woodpecker's behavior of drumming or drilling on the side of a house, shed, garage or barn.

## CHASE THEM AWAY

When possible, tackle the problem as soon as it begins. Use of noise to chase away the birds (including shouting or banging of pans) and the squirting of a hose or a pulsating lawn sprinkler may be effective.

Hang objects that move and reflect light over the damaged area: mylar balloons, children's pinwheels, reflective tape, aluminum pie pans, strips of aluminum foil or Christmas tree tinsel.

When the birds are pecking on your house to get insects, merely hosing down the siding sometimes works, because it may get rid of the insect larvae that the birds are after.

Place scarecrows (such as fake snakes, hawks or owls) near the drilling sites. If they make noise, they will be even more effective.

## EXCLUDE THEM

Nail plywood, metal or plastic sheeting over the bird's excavation sites.

❀ "If they are drilling holes near the eaves in your cedar or redwood siding, you can cover the area with nylon mesh or plastic netting to control damage beneath the eaves," recommended an authority at the Missouri Department of Conservation.

✤ "We had downy woodpeckers working on our cedar siding to get at insects that were in the open grooves," said Martin Rogers, Jackson, Mississippi. "I caulked all the openings I could find and all the holes that the woodpeckers had created, which must have pretty well eliminated that particular source of insects, because we no longer have problems."

## LURE THEM AWAY

If the woodpecker appears to be trying to create a nesting or roosting site, offer a large birdhouse nearby. Flickers or other woodpeckers will often move in, readily deserting their troublesome excavation projects.

Offering food such as suet to woodpeckers may help deter them from drilling for insects in siding.

## REPELLENTS DON'T WORK

More than 50 repellents have been aimed at pesky woodpeckers over the years, but one that actually works has yet to be discovered. As one ornithologist noted, an effective woodpecker repellent exists only in they eye of a con man.

Whatever measures are taken, it should be kept in mind that all woodpeckers are protected by federal and state laws and cannot be killed or injured nor can their nests be disturbed.

# The Nature of the Beast

Downy, hairy, red-headed, red-bellied, flicker and pileated are common woodpeckers that may damage the siding on buildings. The most common of these is the downy, which is also the smallest.

Like other woodpeckers, downies begin their spring drumming as early as January. Their *tap, tap, tap, tap, tap!* is the little black-and-white woodpecker's way of establishing a breeding territory and courting a mate. Males and females are marked the same, except for the red spot on the back of the male's head. The pair court by dancing around tree branches while their wings are raised in tempo with their chattering.

Tree trunks make much better nesting cavities than the siding of your house.

Clinging to a tree, a downy hunts food with jerking movements, pecking the tree with its bill to scale away loose bark in search of wood-boring insects, insect eggs and cocoons. The insect matter consists mostly of economically harmful species such as beetles, caterpillars, weevils and ants. It also eats fruits, as well as weed seeds and crop grains. At bird feeders, downies and other woodpeckers eat suet as well as cracked sunflower seeds and corn.

The downy's bill, like that of other woodpeckers, is chisel-shaped, not pointed as on most other birds. Woodpeckers need that flat chisel tip for carving their nesting and roosting cavities. They also need it to chip away the wood around insects that have bored into tree trunks and siding. Once a woodpecker chisels close to the morsel, its amazing tongue does the rest of the work. Surprisingly long and sticky, twice the length of the bird's head, the woodpecker's tongue has a horny tip of curved barbs used to spear the borers.

That little jackhammer bill also requires a very special skull behind it. Not only is it stronger and thicker than skulls of other birds, it is also heavier. The added weight makes the hammer more effective.

Downies inhabit most of the wooded areas of North America, except for the deserts. They are not deep-forest birds, however, preferring open woodlands, river groves, orchards, swamps, farmlands and suburban backyards.

When the time comes to begin the nesting cycle, the downy female does most of the excavating of the eight- to ten-inch-deep tree cavity, utility pole or side of a building, three to 50 feet above the ground. The four to five white eggs are incubated by both parents, with the male taking the night shift, for 12 days. The young downies are on the wing in about three weeks.

Although no small bird is totally safe from predators, not many downy woodpeckers fall prey to hawks, owls and other winged hunters. When under attack, downies are quite adept at dodging raptors by flitting around the tree trunks and branches of their natural habitat.

By September, the young of the year look like adults, the downy woodpecker family has broken up and all become solitary and quiet.

If the youngsters survive the first year, they will probably live an average of five to seven years in the wild. One banded downy had lived 12 years, five months when it was recaptured, but that was highly unusual.

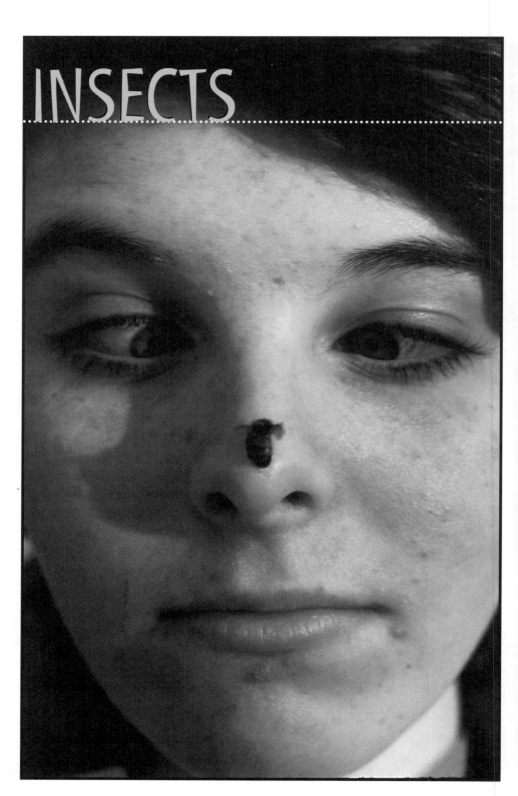

# The Problem with Insects

EVERY SUMMER, HUNDREDS of thousands of Americans are stung by wasps, hornets and bees. Some of these victims are tending bird feeders or birdhouses when they are attacked. Most suffer only burning pain. Some 85,000 others seek medical treatment for allergic reactions and at least 50 of them die, according to the American Academy of Allergy and Immunology.

A birdhouse containing a wasp nest not only keeps birds away, it presents a danger to the unsuspecting backyard birder who opens the birdhouse in the hope of seeing a bird nest or to clean it at the end of the season.

Wasps, hornets and bees are often attracted to hummingbird and oriole feeders that contain sugar water and sometimes to suet feeders. Hummingbirds are easily intimidated by the presence of the belligerent wasps or bees and back off without feeding. The danger to people occurs when the insects are disturbed, as when the feeders are taken down for refilling.

Ants are also a problem at hummingbird and oriole feeders, drawn to the sweet liquid. Feeders covered with ants are often unacceptable to the birds that are meant to feed from them.

# War Stories

✳ "I was taking down the hummingbird feeder to replenish the sugar water when wasps attacked me," reported Alice Jefferson in San Jose, California. "I was stung three times on my hand before I dropped the feeder and ran into the house," she said. "I immediately put ice cubes on the stings, but by that time my hand was already greatly swollen and discolored."

A birdhouse containing a swarm of honey bees.

✳ A 10-year-old boy swallowed a bee when he took a gulp of cola from a can during a backyard picnic in Virginia. He was rushed to a hospital in nearby Front Royal for treatment of an allergic reaction to insect venom.

✳ A hunter in Illinois who sat under his favorite squirrel tree was stung on the hand and face by yellow jackets. He became woozy, confused and had difficulty breathing. His eyes itched and he coughed as a constriction developed in his chest. His heart pounded and he started to sweat profusely. Heading for home, he collapsed and died.

✳ "For years, I had hummingbird feeders in my yard." wrote Margaret Pigg of Marshville, North Carolina. "It seemed that no matter where I put them, ants soon found them and kept the hummingbirds away," she said.

# Solutions

Paradoxically, wasps are efficient predators of many other pest insects. Their diets also include meat, fruits and other sweets, making garbage and picnic areas prime food gathering sites. By keeping tight lids on garbage cans and by picnicking away from garbage, encounters with yellow jackets and other wasps should be limited. For wasps that linger around feeding stations and birdhouses, here are more solutions.

## FIGHT THE STINGERS

❈ One way to reduce the population of wasps, hornets and bees around bird feeders is to trap them. Wasp traps, easily obtainable in stores, are plastic, globe-shaped, covered reservoirs that can be baited with sugar water, meat or fish scraps and hung near the bird feeders to lure the stinging insects inside. Once in, they are unable to find their way out. Dozens may been caught in a single day.

Wasp traps like this will reduce the pesky insects at bird feeders. (Photographed at Mitchell Park Horticultural Conservatory, Milwaukee, Wisconsin.)

❈ "Wasps were pests at my hummingbird feeders, but I solved the problem

An ant moat placed above the hummingbird feeder will keep ants from the sugar water. The plastic cup is commercially available or can be made from the plastic cap of a spray paint can. Bee guards are also inserted at each sugar-water port. (Photographed at Mitchell Park Horticultural Conservatory, Milwaukee, Wisconsin.)

with cooking oil," Betty Rochester of Pine Bluff, Arkansas, wrote in *Birds & Blooms*. "Each time I clean out my feeder, I dip my finger in oil and rub it around the feeding ports. It works," Betty assured. "My feeders have been wasp-free for four years."

❀ Another way to discourage bees and other stinging insects from sugar-water feeders is to mount bee guards on the feeder ports. On hummingbird feeders, bee guards are small, round, plastic grates that slip over the feeding tube, restricting the insects' access but allowing the hummers to feed through the grates with their long bills and tongues. On oriole feeders, bee guards are usually spring-loaded blocks over the feeding holes. An oriole opens a port by lowering the block with its weight as it lands on the feeder.

❀ A wasp nest in a birdhouse should be sprayed with a wasp insecticide and then removed and the house cleaned of the toxins to again make it usable for the birds.

## SPRAY JUDICIOUSLY

❀ To destroy wasps' or yellow jackets' hanging globe-shaped nests, or nests in underground burrows, they may be sprayed, preferably at night, from as far as 12 feet away with an insecticide such as Raid Wasp & Hornet Killer.

As tempting as it may be to spray pesticides at bird feeders, it is ill advised. The pesticides contain toxins that may be harmful to the birds that feed from the ports where the insects would be sprayed.

Wasps' globe-shaped nests may be sprayed, preferably at night, from as far as 12 feet away with an insecticide.

## ANT DEFENSES

❀ Margaret Pigg discovered that the ultimate way to rid her hummingbird feeders of ants was to place a small wooden post in the middle of the recirculating pool in her backyard. Then, she hung her sugar water feeders from the post. "The arrangement really works beautifully," she reported in *Birds & Blooms*. "The ants can't get to the feeders and the hummers are attracted to the trickling water, too."

Another very effective ant controller is a little cup, available commercially from most bird stores, lawn-and-garden centers and hardware stores that is designed to hang between the sugar-water feeder and the hook from which the feeder is suspended. When the cup is filled with water, ants cannot cross over it to get to the feeder.

An option to the water-filled cups is to slather the wire or string holding the feeder with cooking oil or Vasoline. Ants will not cross the oily surface to get to the sugar water.

❀ Make your own ant moat, recommended Charley Sayre of Newark, Ohio. "Most cans of spray paint have a plastic cap with a built-in 'moat' inside," he told the readers of *Birds & Blooms*. Charley drilled a hole slightly smaller than ⅜-inch diameter in the center of the cap. Then he inserted a small screw eye into each end of a 2½- or 3-inch-long ⅜-inch dowel. "Push the dowel through the hole until the cap is centered on it, fill the cap with water and hang the simple ant-stopper above the feeder. It really works," he said.

## FEEDER REPELLENTS

There are some substances that can be applied directly on feeders to destroy insects' ability to smell the sugar water or nectar. Avon's Skin-So-Soft or Vicks VapoRub, for example, can be rubbed on the spouts or around the ports (not in the ports) of the feeders to deter insects from feeding there.

## WHAT TO DO IF STUNG

Four to eight of every 1,000 of us are allergic to the venom of wasps, hornets and bees and a sting could be fatal within 10 to 15 minutes (80 percent of venom-related deaths occur within one hour). That's why insects are responsible for many more deaths annually in the U.S. than snakebite.

If you or a companion ever suffers from such an allergic reaction, the victim should be rushed to a medical center for treatment.

Outdoor people, however, are often a long way from medical help and may require first aid in the field. First, scrape out the stinger with a knife (bees' stingers

A wild bee swarm such as this one in a Florida backyard could be a problem if the bees became aggressive.

A honey bee in goldenrod. If you are stung by a bee, wasp or hornet, watch carefully for allergic reactions. Seek medical help immediately if any symptoms appear.

detach in their victims). Do not pull it out or squeeze it because that will force more venom into the wound. Next, wash and disinfect the sting site. Then apply ice packs and/or a paste of baking soda and water to relieve pain.

Most importantly, be alert for symptoms of an allergic reaction—itching around the eyes, dry, hacking cough, widespread hives, constriction of the chest and throat, wheezing, nausea, abdominal pain, vomiting and dizziness. If they appear, get medical help at once.

If you know you are allergic to insect venom, carry an anti-sting Hollister-Stier Ana-Kit, which includes a syringe preloaded with epinephrine (adrenaline). You'll need a doctor's prescription. Another useful tool is the

Sawyer First Aid Kit, which includes The Extractor, a suction device that removes the venom of insects and snakes. Use After Bite, a dab of ammonia or application of ice to reduce itching and promote healing.

# The Nature of the Beasts

All 4,000 wasp species in the United States have the capacity to sting, yet surprisingly, only a few are a threat to people. That's because nearly all wasps are solitary and inoffensive and they sting solely to paralyze their insect prey. Only members of the subfamily *Vespinae*, which includes yellow jackets, paper wasps and hornets, use their stings primarily for defense and may attack humans.

Where do all the wasps come from? Each spring, a queen yellow jacket emerges from winter hibernation and lays eggs either underground or in a small gray paper globe that she builds. The eggs become workers in a few weeks, allowing the queen to produce more workers, as many as 5,000 per nest, that become food gatherers, feeders of young, nest builders and guards. These are the bees that most often threaten people.

In late summer, the queen lays eggs of a different sort. Some of these are future queens and some are males that will breed with future queens. The young males and queens soon fly out of the nest and mate with those from other nests.

As fall approaches, the males, workers and the old queen all die. The gray paper orb nests are deserted, except for a few corpses of workers. Only the new queens survive to hibernate in a tree cavity through the winter and emerge in spring to start the cycle all over again.

# Index